Murder Most Canadian

An Eye-Opening Look at Some of the
Nation's Most Fascinating Cases

By Aldus Greene

P M

Meager
Press

Dedicated to those who seek the truth, even if it's not comfortable, pleasant or what they thought it would be

Murder Most Canadian
by Aldus Greene

Published by The Meager Press of Toronto,
themeagerpress.com ©2016 The Meager Press

Cover image by Wikimedia Commons

ISBN: 978-0-9939950-6-4

Introduction

My editor thought I was crazy when I told him I wanted to write a book about murder in Canada that did not include Paul Bernardo and Karla Homolka. He was shocked to learn that it didn't have Robert "Willie" Pickton, either. Nor does it include Yves "Apache" Trudeau or Marc Lépine. In fact, most of the stories would be about people who killed one or two people. I have my reasons for not including the more famous killers, and I think it makes Murder Most Canadian a better book.

Bernardo and Homolka aren't here because they are Canada's best known murderers. Their story has been told over and over again, most notably by Nick Pron in his excellent book Lethal Marriage. I really wouldn't have anything significant to add.

Pickton — who was accused of killing 49 women, but charged with just six to speed his trial — is an interesting case to be sure. But it's perhaps too interesting, and deserving of more detail than I can get into here.

For sheer body counts, it's hard to match Trudeau, who admitted to taking part in 43 killings. But his story, as is often the case with professional hit men, is tiresomely repetitive. Somebody gets into debt with drug dealers, they call Trudeau, he kills them, gets paid and the cycle repeats itself.

And as far as Lépine and his ilk are concerned, I think the less time and effort we devote to agenda-driven spree killers the better.

Instead of these stories, there are cases you might not have heard of, and some you probably think you know.

Take, for example, the Evelyn Dick case, made famous by the book and movie both named Torso. If you are familiar with the case, you probably believe that Evelyn was something of a heartless, calculating criminal mastermind, as she has been portrayed for decades. But that's not even close to true. Historical records show that she was developmentally disabled, serially abused and unable to make decisions as an adult. Setting the record straight is one of the reasons I wrote Murder Most Canadian.

Other cases, like that of Dale Nelson — who killed seven people, including four children, in a drunken rage in 1970 — are almost unknown to most Canadians. While others — like the tragic killing of 12-year-old Emanuel Jaques in 1977 — were sensations at the time, but have faded from collective memory. Still others — like Uluksuk, the first Inuit to be charged with murder — have great historic value and help the reader understand how Canada became Canada.

It's a strange lot. Both victims and aggressors transcend all lines of ethnicity, gender, sexual orientation and age. We've got 12-year-old victims and 12-year-old murderers.

Of course, Murder Most Canadian has had to leave out a number of equally fascinating cases. Should it prove popular, a second volume could well be in the offing. That is, if my editor doesn't think it's crazy.

Chapter 1

Medicine Hat Massacre

When Marc Robertson went to pick his daughter up after a January 2006 concert in Medicine Hat, Alberta, he saw pretty much exactly what he didn't want to see. Jade, his 12-year-old, was intensely making out with some guy in the parking lot.

He didn't recognize the guy, but he knew right away he wasn't the kind of boyfriend he wanted for Jade. He was scruffy and unkempt. His head was shaved, except for a few brightly dyed tufts on the side, he wore thick black eyeliner and a spiked dog collar and had plenty of other accessories and attributes fathers generally disapprove of. If Marc had looked closely, he would have noticed that the guy, Jeremy Allan Steinke, also had a vial of what he said was human blood hanging from a chain on his neck.

When he finally got her in the car, Marc, furious, told Jade that she was grounded for at least a month, and she was not allowed to see that boy ever again.

If Marc had known more about Steinke, he would have been even angrier. He wasn't just a little older than Jade, he was 23. He was an unemployed drifter who slept in various friends' places or in a unit in a nearby trailer park that was sort of open to anyone who wanted to use it.

Steinke had a troubled childhood — he was teased incessantly in school, abused by more than one of his mother's male partners — and battled depression and delusion for most of his life.

After the incident, Jade was angry. She thought it was unfair for her to be grounded, especially for that long. Relations between the girl, who looked much older than her 12 years, and her parents were strained.

Her friends in seventh grade noticed a big difference in her after the concert too. She had always been a little adventurous, several of them said, but all she could talk about after the show was the music she now loved — widely reported using the catch-all term punk rock, but it was actually goth-metal, particularly the band Cradle of Filth — and her new boyfriend. They were in love, she said, they were going to get married. She also complained about her parents, who she called "mean" for grounding her.

The other girls were skeptical, but she would occasionally get one of them to lend her a cellphone so she could talk to Steinke at recess. They also kept in touch via social media — her under the name Runawaydevil and him styled as Souleater — something her parents were unaware of. They spoke about their shared wiccan faith, about Cradle of Filth and other bands and about a love for blood.

It was on one of those recess calls — with Jade sitting on a green metal electrical utility box — that the girls, who always listened in on her calls to Steinke, heard her complain about her parents. "I wish they were dead," they heard her tell them "I wish they were out of my life."

Friends say that a change had come of Steinke, too. Even his best friends admitted he could be a pretty weird dude. He frequently claimed that he was not an unemployed 23-year-old high school dropout, but actually a 300-year-old werewolf (although he always called himself a "lycan," short for lycanthrope).

Most people who knew him didn't take his werewolf claims very seriously — one friend described their little group's sentiment about it as "whatever floats your boat" — but Steinke apparently did. Once, when he and a friend were headed out for a walk on a night with a full moon, he warned 22-year-old Daniel Clark — an oil worker and country music fan who knew him, but thought he was a bit nuts — not to go with them.

"I wouldn't suggest it," Steinke told him. "We'll tear you limb from limb."

Surprised, all Clark could say was: "Excuse me?"

"Yeah," he told him. "I'll eat you."

Clark then threatened to bash him in the head with a baseball bat, so they left it at that.

But after the show, Garth Bolt — Steinke's best friend, who lived with him at the Tower Estates trailer park flophouse — noticed him fall into depression and anxiety because Jade was grounded. "He was a completely different person," Bolt told said. "He was very depressed; he didn't seem to care about anything."

In April, Bolt and Steinke had just attended another concert when Steinke went into one of his now-frequent tirades about how much he loved Jade and hated her parents. Bolt had thought he'd heard it all before until it took a turn for the sinister. "Do you think I'm crazy?" he asked. "Should I really go through with this? Is love worth killing for?"

Bolt begged off, saying he didn't want to get involved, but Steinke continued, saying that if he didn't kill Jade's parents, she was going to leave him for good. Still, Bolt did not think Steinke was serious, and when he again asked for help killing them, Bolt answered: "Go fuck yourself."

Jordan Attfield, 19, was staying in the same trailer as Steinke, and knew him, but would not describe himself as a friend — "he scared the hell out of me," he said.

Attfield, who also believes in lycanthropy, said that he had seen Steinke intentionally cut himself and drink the blood, but that "he never drank blood out of a glass or anything."

Earlier in April, he had picked up one of the receivers of the trailer's landline phone. He could hear that Jade and Steinke were talking. For reasons he did not disclose, he did not hang up right away. Attfield heard her say that she couldn't stand to live with her parents anymore and that she wanted to "get rid of them." Steinke, he said, told her that he'd consider it.

A few days later, Steinke asked Attfield if he would help him kill someone. Attfield, sure it was a joke, ignored the request. The following day, Steinke asked again, and Attfield did his best to laugh it off saying "I don't have the balls."

On the morning of April 23, 2006, another of Steinke's friends, who did not want to be named, said Steinke dropped by his apartment for a few drinks and to snort some cocaine.

An underage girl who was also there said that Steinke watched Natural Born Killers — an acclaimed film about a man and his much-younger girlfriend who begin their killing spree by murdering her parents. She also heard him say "I don't want to do this … are you sure you want to do this?" to someone on the telephone.

When the film came to a scene in which a little boy is spared from the murderers, Steinke told the girl: "That's where it would be different; Jade would kill her brother." The girl, fearing Steinke might not be kidding, tried to talk him out of any violence. He told her she didn't understand the situation and left.

A few hours later, Steinke returned to the same friend's place. "He looked pretty beat up," the friend said. He also said that Steinke asked him if he knew anything about cleaning blood off knives.

Not long after that, Bolt stopped by the trailer, and saw Steinke making out with Jade. They stopped when he came in and Steinke opened a bag from a nearby fast food restaurant — he had a hamburger and she had poutine. Another person who was there, 18-year-old Belinda Hope, would later say Jade "seemed really happy."

Knowing something had to be up, Bolt asked Steinke to talk with him outside. Once they were alone, Steinke lifted his sunglasses to show Bolt his right eye, which was swollen and puffy, soon to be a shiner. Bolt asked him how he got it. Steinke explained that Jade's dad had given it to him when he had taken care of her parents. He then explained that her younger brother had to go too.

That was enough for Bolt. He felt dizzy, then sick. He walked away and started to think about telling the police. Steinke, perhaps sensing that, took Jade and looked for a way out of Medicine Hat.

But the police had already been informed. Another Tower Estates denizen who also described himself as Steinke's best friend, James Whalley, had been there when Steinke walked in, wearing sunglasses at night, and Jade arrived by taxi a few minutes later. He said that Steinke had bragged about killing Jade's parents, and said he had "gutted them like a fish." She joined in, pointing out how her brother "gurgled" when his voice box was sliced open.

Whalley described their demeanor as "calm" and their recounting of the events as being "completely like mellow, every-day conversation."

As soon as he thought it was safe to do so, Whalley ran to the police station. "I was frantic," he later said. "I was freaking out; I didn't know what to think — I had a warrant out for my arrest."

***

In the nice parts of Medicine Hat, people don't think about crime that much, so it was not unusual for a 6-year-old to walk around the neighborhood unescorted on a Sunday afternoon. One of them, a little boy, walked over to a nearby house where an 8-year-old boy he knew named Jacob lived. When nobody answered the door, the little guy looked in the basement window and saw two grown-ups lying on the floor in a huge pool of blood. Instinctively, he ran home.

His mother — who had known the Robertsons since they had moved to the house from Ottawa three years earlier — called 911.

Medicine Hat Police Inspector Brent Secondiak responded, convinced it was a false alarm. But when he saw bodies on the floor through the basement window, he called for backup and broke in.

He found Marc with 24 stab wounds, his wife Debra with 12, and their 68-pound 8-year-old son Jacob with stab wounds to his head and chest and slashed throat. All three were dead.

Police quickly established that the couple also had a 12-year-old daughter. She was not found at the scene, and she was declared missing, potentially kidnapped. "I truly believed that this person was missing and possibly abducted," Secondiak told the media. "It wasn't even in the realm of possibility that she was an accused."

Witnesses said they saw a gray 1987 Dodge Dakota truck leave the scene, but Steinke fled the scene on foot. Jade had actually taken Debra's debit card, went to a convenience store to withdraw cash, called a taxi, waited 20 minutes for it to arrive and left for the trailer in it.

Police found disturbing drawings and writings in Jade's room and her school locker. When word of what Bolt and Whalley had told them came down, Jade's status changed from potential abductee to suspect.

While they were at the trailer, one of the people who arrived after them was Steinke's friend Kacey Danielle Lancaster. Steinke asked her if she could drive him and Jade away from Medicine Hat. He explained that Jade was running away from home and that he wanted to go with her. She agreed, in part, because she was helping another friend, a 16-year-old girl, run away from her foster parents.

Steinke recruited them to clean a pickup truck they all frequently used, and Lancaster found what she called an expensive-looking knife inside. Another underage girl who went along on the ride noticed blood on the truck, but later said: "I was stoned, I didn't ask questions."

She, Steinke, Jade, the 16-year-old, another underage girl and Lancaster drove to Leader, Saskatchewan, about 100 miles away. As they were headed into town, Lancaster noticed that the truck's fuel gauge was nearing empty. It was still before sunrise, so she stopped the truck in a field, where the occupants slept, waiting for sunlight and the opportunity to get gas.

After sunrise, they babied the truck to a nearby gas station. They pooled their funds for fuel, but Steinke also picked up a newspaper because the murders were plastered all over the front page. The 16-year-old would-be runaway testified later that Jade used the pictures in the paper to explain to her and Lancaster how she and Steinke killed her family.

Not long after, police surrounded the truck, which was stopped in an otherwise empty parking lot, and the occupants surrendered. Jade, Lancaster said, expressed concern over Steinke because he had "only committed crimes for her," and that he might be charged with rape because she was naked from the waist down when the police arrived.

Jade and Steinke were each charged with three counts of first-degree murder. She was the youngest person in Canadian history to be charged with multiple counts of murder.

Lancaster was charged as an accessory after the fact, and the runaway was charged with obstruction of justice after she snuck a razor into a police car, cut up the upholstery and tried to kick out a window. She later described her actions as "one of those stupid things people do." The other girl was driven home.

The day after they were arrested, Steinke sent Jade a letter from his holding cell that read: "U said you want to get engaged? Then here's a Q ... Will U marry me? If so then it is a verbal agreement!"

She responded with her own letter, that read, in part:

"Ahahaha! I never thought I'd find myself hystericaly laughing in a holding cell in these kinds of circumstances...or ever really. But still! ahaha you make me so happy! Yes! Yes! I will, I would love to… Interesting information I came across. Anything you can say to anyone, including a phycistrist, unless issued by a lawyer can be used against you! For fucks sake. Rawr. The world really is against us."

Their trials were sensational, but the outcome was rarely in doubt. The Crown presented material from the couple's many social media accounts, like a direct message from Jade to Steinke that read: "I have this plan. It begins with me killing them and ends with me living with you."

And another, that Steinke posted to a public forum, that read:

"Payment! My Lover's rents [slang for parents] are totally unfair; they say that they really care; they don't know what is going on the just assume. As their greed continues to consume, she is slowly going insane. She continues to thank that I came, into her life to help her out, and to stop what they keep trying to shout. It's all total bullshit. Their throats I want to slit. They will regret the shit they have done. Especially when I see to it that they are gone. They shall pay for their insulince. Finally there shall be silence. Their blood shall be payment!"

Bolt and Whalley testified against their shared "best friend." So did several others.

It was looking bad for the couple, and then it got worse. An undercover officer who was posing as a suspect sharing a cell with Steinke played a recording in court of a conversation they had just after Steinke was arrested. In it, he said:

"The last thing I really remember was him … and after him attempting to stab me, fuck, him laying on the ground asking me why and I said 'cause you treat your daughter like shit; she wanted it this way, and, shit, and that was it and then I went upstairs and I watched my girlfriend cut her brother's throat. [Indiscernible word] it didn't bother her at all either, she didn't cry or anything. In fact, the next day, when we were on the road, shit, she was laughing about it. She's got a few screws loose too."

At that point, Steinke kind of gave up, admitting that he had gone into the Robertsons' basement, surprised Debra and began stabbing her. Marc had rushed down the stairs at the sound of screaming and, on seeing Steinke, punched him in the face, Steinke responded by stabbing Marc to death. Marc grabbed his own knife, but was already too far gone. The last words he would ever hear were: "It's what your daughter wanted."

Then Steinke went upstairs. He found Jade trying to choke her frantic little brother. She testified that Steinke shouted: "Stab him! Stab him! Slit his throat!"

She said she couldn't. "You have to," he snapped and then showed her the blood on his knives and clothes. "I did this for you!"

With her left hand still clutching Jacob, she accepted the knife. The little boy screamed "I'm scared! I'm too young to die!" as she stabbed him in the chest.

Shocked, she then dropped the knife. Steinke grabbed it and slashed the throat of the screaming boy, silencing him forever.

But, after recounting the horrific few minutes in which three innocent people had been brutally murdered, Steinke rationalized his actions that day, citing true love. "I never thought that I'd actually kill anybody, but when, once I found my, my soul mate, my true love," he said. "I just, for some reason, I was willing to do anything for her."

Steinke's defense, led by Alain Hepner, was two-pronged. He argued that Steinke had been drunk and stoned at the time, and that his life had been so miserable up to the point at which he met Jade, that he acted impulsively. Hepner called him "a young man with zero self-esteem who finally found someone to love him." Steinke's mother, Jacqueline May, tearfully testified (always with a Bible in her hands) that her son had been abused by several of her boyfriends and that he had been on antidepressants and anti-ADHD medicine since his early teens.

When judge and jury looked unmoved, Steinke claimed that he had tried to talk Jade out of the killings, but that she would not take no for an answer.

At her own, earlier, trial, in which much of the same evidence was presented, Jade claimed she was "kidding" and had no idea Steinke was actually serious about the killings.

Jade was found guilty on all three counts, and was given the maximum sentence for someone her age tried as an adult — 10 years, minus credit for 18 months already served. Since she completed five years of day release without being charged with any crimes, Jade received a complete pardon, and the murders have been expunged from her record. It's as if she was never involved, although she is not legally allowed to own firearms for the rest of her life, and she was required to submit a DNA sample to the national database.

Steinke was also found guilty on all three counts, and was given three concurrent life sentences with no chance at parole for 25 years.

Jade, by all accounts, responded well to rehabilitation. She broke up with Steinke soon after her sentence was read. Her handlers said that she showed genuine remorse and was eager to start a new life.

They pointed out that she had acheived a better than 90 percent grade average on her remote high school classes. In spite of the fact that she was diagnosed with both conduct disorder and oppositional defiant disorder, she was deemed to be at low risk to reoffend.

Upon her release in 2011, Queen's Bench Justice Scott Brooker told her: "I think your parents and brother would be proud of you. Clearly you cannot undo the past; you can only live each day with the knowledge you can control how you behave and what you do each day."

She has since been accepted into an upper-echelon university and has faded into obscurity under a new identity. People on the internet occasionally try to track her down, but without much success.

Steinke appealed his sentence, but later abandoned the process when it became apparent it would not go his way. At his appeal, he announced that he had changed his name to Jackson May.

Lancaster pleaded guilty to obstruction of justice and received a one-year conditional sentence with no jail time.

Note: *Even though she has gone in and out of the system and been given a new identity, Canadian law dictates that I cannot use Jade Robertson's real name. Her name was publicly used when an Amber Alert was issued while it was still unclear if she was missing or involved, and her name has been frequently published in accounts of the story in other countries and online, but in Canada, she was always referred to in media simply as JR. Instead, I have used a similar name both for Jade and her deceased family.*

Chapter 2

Collateral Damage

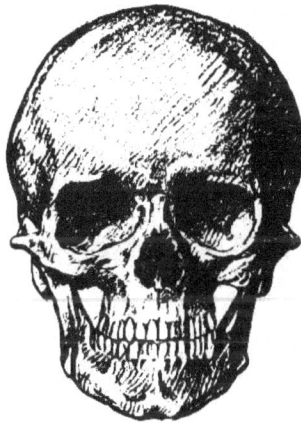

It was just another boring morning for five men repairing the Canadian National Railway tracks in the woods outside Sault-au-Cochon, Quebec, until they heard an explosion.

Instinctively, the men — two of them combat veterans from the Second World War — looked up into the sky where the sound had come from. They saw a Canadian Pacific DC-3 smoking but not aflame falling from the sky.

Seconds later, the doomed airplane smashed into the side of Cap Tourmente, a tree-covered mountain nearby.

Without hesitation, the men — and another who was fishing on the St. Lawrence at the time and also saw the plane go down — ran through the thick forest to the crash site.

What they found there was more horrific than they could have imagined. It was a time before seatbelts were commonplace and all of the passengers and crew had been thrown forward into a massive heap of bodies and parts. "Arms, legs, severed heads ... lying around on the ground," one of the would-be rescuers later told the media. "The forward part of the plane looked intact. The bodies were piled up in there as if they had been thrown forward when the plane crashed. There was nothing we could do, so we rushed out of the woods to alert the railway authorities."

Flight 108, from Montreal to Baie-Comeau with a short stopover at Quebec City's L'Ancienne-Lorette airport, had crashed at 10:46 a.m. on Friday, September 9, 1949. All 23 people aboard, including four children, were killed on impact.

Among the more flamboyant mourners was Quebec City's Joseph-Albert Guay, who usually went by the name Albert. At the elaborate funeral for his wife, Rita, the centerpiece was a five-foot floral cross with a sash that read "From your beloved Albert." He was so overtaken with grief, it appeared, that he tearfully told a priest "if this is what God wants, I just have to accept it."

A neighbor of the Guays' — Roger Lemelin, who just happened to be the Quebec correspondent for Time magazine and who knew that the couple were having marital problems — attended the funeral and told the distraught-looking Albert that he had heard that someone had planted a bomb on the plane. Albert appeared shocked. "I don't believe it," he told Lemelin. "There's nobody monstrous enough to blow up a plane."

Clearly, there was. Despite his guise of grief, Guay was secretly delighted. He'd set out to kill his wife, collect on her insurance and marry his young girlfriend — and it looked like he'd gotten away with it.

People who knew Guay later told the media that he was something of a spoiled brat. The youngest of five children, he had always been treated as special by his parents. Even as an adult, he was prone to fits of temper when he didn't get his way and could be cruel and vindictive.

But he wasn't without charm. Albert was a door-to-door jewelry salesman and had an enviable level of success. He also used his slickness to acquire a young girlfriend, 17-year-old nightclub waitress Marie-Ange Robitaille. At first, Albert would meet her at her parents' house, introducing himself as Robert Angers to hide the fact that he was married.

Albert's marriage had been struggling for years. Married with a flourish in 1940, by 1945, he and Rita Guay (formerly Rita Morel) opened a shop and had a daughter. The shop did not do great business and contemporary reports in the media claimed that the petty Albert could not stand to see someone in the family get more attention than he did, and his resentment of his daughter drove him to despise Rita.

About two years after the affair began, Rita found out about it and went to the Robitailles' house to confront the couple and tell her parents. Outraged, the Robitailles threw Marie-Ange out of the house and said they never wanted to see her or Albert ever again.

Albert quickly moved Robitaille into a house owned by Marguerite Pitre. She was a sister of Généreux Ruest, a friend and client of Albert's who made jewelry and watches. Pitre was a large, almost obese, and stern-looking woman who always wore black, earning herself the nickname Madame le Corbeau (Mrs. Raven) in her neighborhood.

Marie-Ange was unhappy there, and when word spread of their affair, she wanted to leave town. So Albert rented her an apartment in Sept-Îles, and commuted between his wife and job and his girlfriend 300 miles down the St. Lawrence.

Neither woman, of course, was happy with the arrangement. Marie-Ange threatened to leave him, so Albert bought her an expensive engagement ring.

Rita had an affair of her own, and when Albert found out, he was so incensed that he bit deeply into her cheek in an effort to scar her so badly that no man would ever find her attractive again.

Although the two hated each other, they stayed together. Not only did they have a little girl to raise and a business to run, but divorce was essentially impossible for Quebeckers at the time.

Overcome by stress and mounting debts, Albert decided to kill Rita.

He approached an old drinking buddy who he knew had a shady past and offered him $500 to poison the cherry wine she often enjoyed. The man refused, but did not report him to the authorities for fear of what Albert knew about him.

Rebuffed, Albert waited until he could come up with a better plan. When he read in a newspaper that a woman in the Philippines and five accomplices had tried to murder her husband by placing a bomb on board an airplane he was going to fly in later that day, he thought it was a brilliant plan. The Filipino conspirators had been caught at the airport, but Albert thought he was smarter than them.

He knew exactly who to see to build the bomb. Ruest was not only an old friend, but he also owed Albert a lot of money. Besides, nobody would suspect him. Although he was still very productive and a master builder, Ruest's pelvis had been destroyed by osseus tuberculosis and he had severely limited mobility, even with a wheelchair.

But while Ruest was an excellent craftsman and Albert had spent all of the Second World War working for Canadian Arsenals, a munitions factory, neither of them knew how to make a bomb. So they went to a local hardware store — explosives, firearms and ammunitions were freely available at retail stores throughout Canada back then — and asked the owner how to make a bomb. They told him that they were planning to construct a fish pond and needed a quick way to make a big hole. The helpful hardware guy instructed them the on basics of bomb-building, and Ruest quickly put it all together. But to keep from leaving too obvious a trail, they didn't buy anything from that store.

Instead, they recruited Pitre, Ruest's sister. She went to a different hardware store and, using a story about blowing up a gigantic tree stump she had been unable to uproot, bought 20 sticks of dynamite, blasting caps, some batteries and an alarm clock.

Satisfied his friend could build an effective explosive device, Albert convinced Rita that he needed her to fly up to Baie-Comeau to get a collection of gemstones he had bought. Eager to get away from him, even just for a few days, she agreed.

Albert drove her to the airport early Friday morning, and bought a $10,000 life insurance policy on her. Rita also already had a $5,000 insurance policy. Although it might seem suspicious today, buying life insurance policies at the airport was much more common back then — they were even sold from vending machines — when people were less secure with the idea of air travel. But it was interesting that he only bought insurance for the flight to Baie-Comeau and not for the flight back.

At about the same time, Pitre arrived at the airport and paid to have a large box sent to Baie-Comeau on the same flight. She said that package was fragile and that it was urgently needed at the downriver mining town.

The bomb had been set to ignite precisely 16 minutes after the flight's 10:30 scheduled departure time. Albert calculated that the DC-3 would be over a wide section of the St. Lawrence when the bomb exploded, which he believed would eliminate the chances of anyone surviving and would also send any evidence to the murky river's cold bottom.

Unfortunately for him, though, the flight was delayed by five minutes, and the plane went down over dry land. There were no survivors — one contemporary media report claimed that the only recognizable face in the pile of bodies was Rita's — but there was plenty of material evidence.

Among the debris, amazingly, was a big part of the box Pitre had put the dynamite inside. Researchers Jean-Marie Roussel and Robert Péclet of Montreal's Laboratoire de médecine légale et de police technique determined that the bomb had been constructed in such a way that the blast went in one direction. Luckily for the police, it was away from the would-be receiver's name and address.

The name and address were fictitious, but it still helped the investigation. When detectives showed it to the shipping clerk at the L'Ancienne-Lorette airport, he immediately recognized it and described the woman in black who had sent it. She did not, he said, give her name.

The cops then questioned all the taxi drivers who frequently made trips to the airport, and one told them he distinctly remembered driving the woman in black. He remembered her as testy, and recalled that she told him to avoid any bumps or sharp turns because "these aren't eggs I'm carrying."

The investigators then went to the neighborhood she was picked up in and started asking questions. It wasn't long before several people identified the woman in question as Madam le Corbeau.

After a long interrogation, Pitre told them that Albert had given her the package to take to the airport, but she swore that she had no idea what was inside.

While the police were watching Albert and trying to build a case against him, they learned that Pitre had attempted suicide by swallowing a large number of sleeping pills.

When she woke up the following day on September 23, her hospital bed was surrounded by cops. Succumbing to the pressure or guilt, she came clean. She said that she knew the package contained a bomb and that it was intended to kill Rita.

Pitre also explained that, when he found out that the cops had interviewed her, Albert convinced her to take her own life. He even had her write a note that read: "Do not look for the guilty one. I am dead. I did it. I wanted to destroy Mrs. Guay."

That was enough. The cops swooped in on Albert and arrested him and charged him with multiple counts of murder.

Albert's trial in February 1950 was a media sensation, but more or less an open-and-shut case. The jury took all of fifteen minutes to find him guilty. He was sentenced to death.

After the verdict was read, Albert admitted his guilt and implicated Ruest and Pitre. More than one media observer opined that it appeared to be a cynical attempt on Albert's part to delay or even overturn his death sentence. It didn't work.

Both conspirators were arrested in June 1950. Ruest was tried first. He claimed that Albert told him first that the bomb was necessary to clear some fields of stumps and then later in the same trial that the pair had planned to go "dynamite fishing."

But after a witness testified that he had seen Ruest painfully lift himself out of his wheelchair on an observation deck of the Chateau Frontenac to watch the flight go by, the jury found him guilty. He, too, was sentenced to be hanged.

Albert's testimony in Ruest's trial differed little from the statements he had made earlier, and his participation in Pitre's trial was not deemed essential since he had already stated his case against her.

He was executed on January 12, 1951. The hangman later told the media that Albert's last words were "Au moins, je meurs célèbre (At least I die famous)."

On July 25, Ruest was wheeled up to the same Montreal gallows, and then carried by two men up the steps, propped up as a noose and hood were placed over his head and he was hanged.

At her own trial, Pitre recanted everything she had said from her hospital bed and claimed that Albert had told her that the box contained a statue. The jury did not believe her.

Pitre, Madam le Corbeau, was hanged five minutes after midnight on January 9, 1953. She was the last woman in Canada to suffer capital punishment.

Chapter 3

Tragedy on the Yonge Street Strip

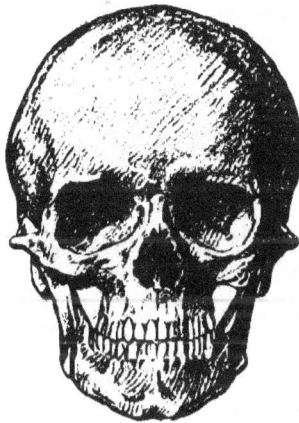

The cultural changes of the middle twentieth century hit Toronto hard. People from the city that had forced movie theaters to stay shut on Sundays until 1961, and wouldn't allow bars to be open on the Sabbath until a year after that, would hardly recognize their town just a few years later. By the middle 1970s, it was a very different place than the city that liked to call itself "Toronto the Good" — sometimes sarcastically.

The epicenter of that change was the Yonge Street strip. Long a place of commerce and culture, it had become kind of a Sin City unto itself. Although the Metropolitan Toronto government had helped with the recent construction of the massive Eaton Centre mall on the strip (in no small part to help bring a little stability to the area), in 1977 the short stretch of Yonge between Adelaide and Bloor still featured 31 "nude encounter" massage parlors, two dozen porn cinemas, six adult bookstores and, according to a contemporary report by the Globe and Mail: "in addition to strip-tease and live sex shows, there is one parlor that guarantees that its female attendants will masturbate customers as part of the $25 entrance fee."

There wasn't a lot the cops could do about it either. The maximum penalty allowed by law for operating what was then called a "common bawdy house" was just $500. The time and effort it took to prosecute didn't make it worth their while — especially since the establishments would just re-open the following day if they even closed at all.

Along with the employees and customers of these businesses, Yonge Street attracted street prostitutes and pimps, drug dealers and addicts, the mentally unhealthy, the curious, the criminal and many, many others.

Young people hung out there, business people from downtown passed through on their way uptown or to the suburbs, and there was a small army of child laborers who did their best to cater to the needs of the people there. Some sold newspapers, others sold cigarettes (illegal for several reasons, but generally tolerated) and others shined shoes. Some were prostitutes. Some just begged.

It was a dangerous place, everybody knew that, but still they came. Some were sent by immigrant parents who not only needed the extra money, but sincerely believed that the work nurtured an entrepreneurial spirit and the adversity built a strong character.

Emanuel Jaques was 12 in the summer of 1977, and he wanted to go to Yonge Street. The family had emigrated from Portugal's Azores Islands three years earlier and weren't exactly well off. They lived in a small but tidy government-subsidized house at 410 Shuter Street that has since been demolished to make way for the Regent Park Community Centre.

The family encouraged little Emanuel — who was slight and looked more like he was 9 or 10 than his 12 years — and his siblings to work, but not on Yonge Street. They didn't want their kids seeing those things, being with those people.

Instead, Emanuel sold flowers on Queen Street and generally made $10 to $15 a day. But he knew that his big brother Luciano and his pal Shane McLean made a lot more from shining shoes on Yonge.

His parents were firm, but Emanuel persisted. He would be safe, he said. All his friends went to Yonge Street and they made way more money than him. Besides, the cops had caught him selling on Queen Street without a vendor's permit and, although they did not give him a ticket, they told him not to come back.

He also pointed out that the family was planning a trip back to the Azores later that summer, and Emanuel wanted to look good in front of his old friends and relatives. Finally, his father, Valdemito, and his mother, Maria, relented and let him go shine shoes on Yonge Street. Emanuel made his own wooden shoe shine kit and painted it pale green.

But on July 28, he didn't come home. His frantic parents called police.

At the time, lots of kids ran away to Yonge Street, seduced by its seedy attractions, and some of them became prostitutes. But it was quickly clear to law enforcement that Emanuel wasn't that kind of boy. He had a happy, stable home life with loving parents. He did well in school, was not at all shy about planning for his future and didn't seem to be bullied. It was clear to the police that Emanuel had not run away.

Luciano told them what happened that night. The boys had been working near the stone arch at Granby and Yonge, just south of College, when they were approached by a tall, dark-haired man in construction overalls.

The man struck up a conversation with the boys and offered Emanuel a job. He had some photographic equipment up the street that he needed to have moved upstairs. It was too big a job for him to do himself, so he'd pay the boy $35 to be his helper. He said that if Emanuel did a good job, there could be as much as $400 in it for him.

Luciano said that his little brother was excited to make that much money so quickly, and was pleading with him to allow him to go. It was just a couple of blocks away, Emanuel said. Luciano told his brother that it wasn't up to him, that they would have to ask their parents. While Luciano was trying to get his parents on a payphone, his little brother left with the man. Luciano never saw Emanuel again.

The police asked Luciano to describe the man and they had a sketch artist come up with a composite illustration.

The cops informed the media, and quickly what seemed like the whole city — moved by the photos of the wide-eyed and innocent-looking kid they saw in the newspapers and on TV – was looking for Emanuel.

But it was to no avail. Days passed, and no trace of the boy could be found. Public interest began to wane as it seemed like the boy would never turn up.

One Torontonian who had been watching the case unfold and desperately hoping the boy would be found alive and unharmed was George Hislop.

One of the first prominent LGBQT activists in Toronto history — he was eulogized years later as "Canada's official homosexual" — Hislop was well-known and respected in both political and social circles. It was not uncommon for people in Toronto's LGBQT community to approach him for help or advice, even if they had not met him before.

So, when Hislop answered his phone on July 31, a few days after the disappearance of Emanuel, he was not surprised to hear a voice he did not recognize, one that he could easily tell was full of desperation.

It was Saul David Betesh, a go-go dancer and sex worker who frequented the Yonge Street strip. He told Hislop that he had done a bad thing, and that there was no one else he could turn to. Hislop told him to calm down. He promised would listen and he would try to help him.

He was shocked when Betesh told him that he had killed Emanuel. Hislop knew he had to do what was right not just for the boy and his family, but also for the man on the other end of the line. Without trying to alarm him, Hislop asked Betesh what had happened.

Betesh told him that he and his friends tricked Emanuel into their apartment above the Charlie's Angels massage parlor and peep-show theater at 245 Yonge. He'd struck up a conversation with the boy, and offered him $35 to help him carry some camera equipment up to the second floor.

Once he got the boy upstairs, Betesh locked the door behind them, he and three of his friends raped the boy repeatedly, taking photos all the while, and — as he said they had done before — drugged their victim with sleeping pills, intending to release him somewhere far away.

But the sleeping pills didn't seem to work, and so Betesh decided to kill the boy. He tried to strangle him, but it wasn't working, so he recruited one of the friends to help him drown him in a sink.

Aghast, and hoping that someone was playing an elaborate prank on him, Hislop first arranged for Betesh to get legal representation. The lawyers he knew usually handled smaller stuff, but he knew a guy who could help. Then he persuaded Betesh to give himself up to police. After hanging up, Hislop called the Metropolitan Toronto police and told them what he knew, although he did not name Betesh, trusting him to turn himself in.

The following day, 26-year-old Betesh walked into the headquarters of 51 Division on Shuter Street near Yonge and turned himself in. When the cops asked him why he surrendered, he told them that the artist's sketch he saw in the paper looked enough like him that he figured it was only a matter of time before he was caught.

He wrote a confession that included his description of the actual killing:

"I went in and I put the stretch cord, stretch plastic to hold suitcases onto a car, around his neck and I started to choke him, and it lasted about two or three minutes, and I just couldn't finish the job. I came out and by that time Joe suggested trying to put a pillow over his head so that I couldn't see him and so be able to finish the job. Stretch and I went back in and we decided to drown him so we did it that way."

They asked him where the body was. Betesh told him that they wrapped the boy's corpse in two plastic garbage bags and a shower curtain and hid it under some old rotting lumber and garbage on the roof of 245 Yonge. In an effort to get rid of any other incriminating evidence, they smashed the boy's shoe shine kit and dropped it down the building's chimney.

Cops were dispatched to the scene of the crime. "The place was so filthy inside; with just some old chairs and a screen cut in the wall," one of the detectives told reporters. "There was nothing clean or slick about it — just sheer filth." A search of the premises discovered Emanuel's clothes, some photographic equipment and a pile of photographs. They showed more than a dozen different boys

— some as young as 7 and many of them tied up — nude or even engaging in sex acts. When the film in the camera was developed, almost all of it was ruined, but the two photos that did turn out featured a nude Emanuel with Betesh.

On the roof, just as Betesh had said they would, they found Emanuel's remains. "It was horrible," said Detective Bob McLean, who was one of the cops on the roof that day. "I had a son the same age."

He told them what had happened and also implicated his friends Albert Wayne "Stretcher" Kribs, 41; Josef "Crazy Joe" Woods, 26; and Werner "Gypsy" Gruener, 28. Betesh told the police that the other men who were in the apartment that night — all of whom worked at least occasionally for Charlie's Angels — were feeling the heat and were desperate to get out of Toronto. They were headed, he said, to Vancouver, near where Gruener was originally from.

There was only one train that went from Toronto to Vancouver — the Super Continental — and the OPP found it and stopped it in the tiny Northern Ontario town of Sioux Lookout. Kribs, Woods and Gruener were taken from the train and charged with murder.

When what happened to the boy became front-page news, there was a massive backlash against the already embattled LGBQT community in Toronto. People all over the country quickly become convinced that Toronto was crawling with gay gangs, preying on children. Mass anti-gay demonstrations took place all over Metro Toronto, and several politicians received anti-gay rights petitions with thousands of signatures.

"The gay community is as appalled by this murder as any other group in the city," Hislop said when calls to talk radio and letters to the editor were clearly after his head. "I am being made to share the guilt of the killers, but I am not guilty at all and shouldn't be treated as such."

When Bestesh's identity to revealed, there were several anti-Semitic demonstrations as well.

The trial revealed the quartet all to be deeply damaged men. Betesh, the group's ringleader, was tall and relatively attractive, according to news reports, but severely troubled.

He had been adopted as a baby by a wealthy Jewish family, but it hadn't turned out well for them. Although they provided him with just about everything a kid could want — private school, tutors, sports and music lessons — he was clearly disturbed. When he was 5, he poured a bottle of nail polish remover into his babysitters' ear. It was just one incident in a long line of cruelties he had inflicted on friends, family and pets that included throwing knives at his sister and once trying to electrocute his whole family while they sat in a pool. His parents knew something was wrong with him and sent him to a psychiatrist.

It didn't help. Betesh was kicked out of every school he ever attended (often because he came armed with razors or other weapons) and by 17, he was unemployed and in and out of institutions his family hoped would help him. When asked what he was like at home, his mother testified that he was prone to violence. "We feared for our lives," she said. "We locked ourselves into the bedroom at night, we were so scared."

Betesh summed up his mental state by saying: "I never really liked anybody."

Unable to find work, he started prowling the Yonge Street strip. Tall, young and not bad looking, Betesh found it easy to make money as a dancer, stripper and prostitute. But he began to tire of sex with the nonstop lineup of old men who were his clients. For fun, he had sex with younger men and boys, and found that his tastes ran to the very young.

He met Kribs in the middle 1970s at a gay-rights rally in the neighborhood. Betesh and the 6-foot-5, long-bearded Kribs hit it off right away. They had plenty in common. They were both sex workers. While Betesh plied his trade on the street, Kribs worked at Charlie's Angels.

Born in Windsor to a father who worked on a Ford assembly line and a stay-at-home mother, Kribs also had a trouble childhood. He left school and home at 14, and rode the rails doing odd jobs and petty thefts to get by.

He had problems with his anger, and was quick to turn to violence when things didn't go his way. One woman who knew him, described him in court as a "beast."

At first, Betesh and Kribs shared their interests in CB radios (which were popular at the time) and war-oriented board games. After they got to know each other a little better, they revealed that they both preferred sex with boys over men.

That shared secret created a tighter bond between the two, and Kribs offered to let Betesh stay at his apartment above Charlie's Angels and revealed that he augmented his earnings at the rub and tug by taking pictures of boys and selling them at shops on Yonge Street.

Kribs introduced Betesh to Woods. He too, was into CB radios and war gaming, but spent most of his time dabbling in the occult and taking a lot of drugs. His odd behavior led to him earning the nicknames 'Crazy Joe" and the "Mad Scientist."

He, too, had trouble in school, leaving it and his home in Sudbury after seventh grade.

Although his lawyer would later say that Woods was not attracted to boys — instead preferring, in the parlance of the time, "drag queens" — testimony from a long string of boys who said he had sex with them indicated otherwise. Big, strong and always ready to throw a punch, he worked at Charlie's Angels as a doorman. It was his job to straighten out any client who made trouble or stiffed a worker.

Gruener also worked, at least occasionally, at Charlie's Angels, and frequently slept in the apartment above it. He was called Gypsy because he always seemed to be on the move — usually on his beloved and intricately decorated bike — and he often spoke of places he'd been or would like to visit.

Born in Germany, he had grown up in British Columbia with parents who were very deeply committed to a controversial religious organization then called The Children of God (later the Family of Love and now The Family International). Gruener's mother had suffered what he called a "nervous breakdown" when he was a young teen and attempted suicide. He said it affected him a great deal.

Gruener did very poorly in school — he was held back four times — and left when he was 18. Although he remained on good terms with his parents, he left B.C. for the Toronto area when he was 21.

Once there, he got in trouble frequently, and had several minor brushes with the law.

Friends almost unanimously acknowledged that Gruener was intellectually challenged, and that he had a habit of avoiding stressful situations.

On the first day of the trial, Kribs surprised all in attendance by pleading guilty to first-degree murder.

Although very rare, it was not an unprecedented move. Several attorneys have told me that it usually happens when a defendant is so overcome with guilt that he or she would rather not live through the details again by fighting his or her way through a trial.

The judge asked Kribs if his lawyer had described the seriousness of such an action — a guilty plea to first-degree murder automatically resulted in the stiffest penalty under Canadian law, a life sentence with no chance of parole for 25 years. "Yes he has," Kribs replied. "I know what it is. I am ready to accept it."

The next defendant to appear was Gruener. He carried a Bible with him, and claimed to have not had a clear idea of what exactly happened on the night of Emanuel's death.

The Crown wanted to challenge his credibility. He asked how a deeply religious man like him could work at a place like Charlie's Angels. Gruener replied that he was not sure that anything sinful happened there. And, if it did, it was none of his business. The Crown countered that surely Gruener knew that more than massages were going on in the private booths, but Gruener maintained that he was simply there to make a few bucks and that it was not his concern what other people did there.

The Crown then asked him about his fondness for 12- to 14-year-old girls — something several witnesses had mentioned about him. Gruener countered that his dealings with them were not in any way less than chaste. "I liked talking to little girls, but there was nothing sexual about it," he testified. "I enjoy their company; we get along good."

He then recounted his observations from the night of the murder. He had been in the apartment watching an episode of Three's Company when he heard a knock at the back door, which opened onto a paved alley called O'Keefe Lane.

It was Betesh, who had a little boy with him that Gruener later learned was Emanuel. He let them in, and Betesh said something about taking pictures as he led the boy upstairs.

He didn't really get involved with what was going on with the boy, he testified, instead spending his time sleeping, watching TV and packing for his upcoming trip to see his parents in B.C. He left twice during Emanuel's stay in the apartment to get something to eat at a nearby restaurant.

When the Crown asked him if he saw the boy being raped or abused, he said he didn't, but he did admit that, through an open door while passing a bedroom, he saw the boy tied up and handcuffed to a bed. The Crown asked if he found that shocking, and Gruener responded that he knew Kribs liked to take pictures of the boys he met, so he thought it was part of that.

Gruener said he woke up at about 3 in the morning that night because he could hear the three other defendants arguing about something. He stepped into the living room, and heard them discussing what they should do with the boy. Gruener testified that he told them to take him home to his parents.

The following morning, he said, he saw Kribs and asked him what he did about the boy. Kribs, he testified, told him he took him home.

He then told the court that he had no idea the boy was dead until he was charged with first-degree murder.

He was eventually acquitted.

Things did not go as smoothly for Woods and Betesh. They had little recourse but to listen to the charges against them and to Toronto Police Sergeant Paton Weir reading from the confession Betesh had made on August 1, after turning himself in.

His first remarks indicated that the rest of the gang was aware that Betesh had intended to bring Emanuel back to the apartment. "Everyone was in on it," he said. "They knew I was coming up with the kid."

He actually said that it was Kribs who had seen Emanuel first, and told Betesh that he would be an ideal candidate for photos. "Stretcher saw a shoeshine boy he was interested in," Betesh admitted.

Once they had focused their attention on one potential victim, they discussed strategy. "We talked about how we'd get him up," he continued. "We decided I'd get one using the photography ploy." The men had offered money to boys in exchange for modeling for photos many times before with frequent success.

At first, Emanuel declined, afraid his parents would find out, but later relented. Betesh also told them that the boy admitted to having "hustled" "one or two times" for $15.

Betesh then told the police that he went to the apartment, but couldn't get in. "I picked up Manuel and took him to the body rub," he admitted. "No one was there so we went for dinner at the Howard Johnson's." Emanuel, he said, had a burger and fries.

When he tried the apartment's back door again, Gruener let them in. "When we came back, Werner was there," Betesh said. "He opened the back door so no one would see us go up." Gruener wasn't alone. "By the time we got there, Stretcher and Joe were there too," continued Betesh.

As they had before, the men kept up the act that it was just an ad hoc modeling gig. "I brought him in and we had coffee," he said. "We went into the bedroom and took pictures of him for about an hour; he had all of his clothes on at first."

But then things began to get sexual. "Bit by bit, we got him to take them off until he was nude," Betesh admitted. "We wanted some action shots — and he said no at first — but then Stretcher offered him another $20."

The men, as they said they had before, decided that it was time to rape the defenseless model they had lured upstairs. It did not go as easily as they hoped, so they resorted to extreme measures.

"Stretcher wanted to have intercourse with the kid, but intercourse was too painful for him, so we tied him up and Stretcher and I had intercourse."

Gruener stayed out of the way the whole time.

They had done the same thing to other boys, and had a well-established modus operandi. Once they were through with the boys, they would drug them with sleeping pills and release them, unconscious, far away from the apartment. They depended on the child either not remembering what happened, thinking that the drugs had caused him to dream what happened or, far more likely, just be too ashamed to tell anyone what happened.

But Emanuel was different. Despite his small size, the sleeping pills seemed to have no effect on him. They waited and waited, and his eyes still wouldn't shut. They began to get worried, and Betesh took a needle full of prescription sedatives and injected it into Emanuel's arm.

But still he stayed conscious. They decided they had to kill him. He was Betesh's find, so the responsibility fell on him to do the job. He was their leader, anyway.

Betesh then took a bungee cord and wrapped it around the boy's neck. He pulled tight, but realized he couldn't finish the job. It wasn't that Betesh wasn't strong enough to snuff the life out of the tiny boy, but — in a rare sign of humanity — he couldn't do the job because Emanuel was looking at him.

Kribs, he testified, suggested using a pillow; that way, he said, Betesh wouldn't have to see his eyes.

Woods motioned toward the kitchen sink and said "I think the kid needs a shampoo."

Nobody ever did dishes in the apartment, but the clogged sink was always full of them and water from its dripping faucet. Betesh admitted in court that he took the boy to it, and held his head under the filthy water. Woods held Emanuel's bound legs. After a few moments, the kicking stopped, and then so did the bubbles. Emanuel was dead.

The men then did a round of cleaning to get rid of evidence (they did a poor job, considering the photos were still on film in one of Kribs' cameras and they left Emanuel's clothes there, although Betesh did find time to remove the three one-dollar bills Emanuel had earned that night).

They took the plastic-wrapped body upstairs with plans of shoving it down the chimney, but it was too big, so they covered it with garbage instead.

At the trial, Woods' lawyer, George Marron, tried to paint him as deluded, and damaged by drugs. He claimed that Woods believed he could rob banks by shooting a laser through their doors, that he could kill pigeons in the park with a machine he had made from parts from a microwave and that he could hypnotize people. Several people who knew him testified that he had tried to hypnotize them, but failed. Woods also claimed he had invented a device called the Psytron that he could use to control people's thoughts.

A jury found Betesh and Woods guilty. Betesh was given the same sentence as Kribs. Woods, found guilty of second-degree murder, was given life with no chance at parole for 18 years.

Judge Arthur William Maloney seemed to be as caught up in the anti-gay hysteria as many other Torontonians, and said:

> "There is one feature in your case that disturbs me more
> than a little. It is your acknowledged tendency to seek out
> ever younger homosexual partners. I wonder how
> common that is among homosexuals. There are those who
> seek protections for homosexuals in the Human Rights
> Code. You make me wonder if they are not misguided."

But while the hatred and blame the LGBQT community in Toronto experienced during and after the trial began to wane, tolerance for illegal sex trade businesses on Yonge Street evaporated.

While the cops could only fine the establishments, they could arrest their employees and customers. Night after night, the businesses were raided. Clients, not wanting to get their name in the paper or explain to wives and families why they had to go to court or be bailed out of jail, stayed away in droves. Sex trade employees, who had long treated such arrests as little more than a nuisance, were now facing off against judges who were denying them bail, which was legal after the second arrest for the same offense.

Without workers or customers, it was impossible to make money selling sex on Yonge Street anymore. Before the trial even ended, the cops had managed to close A Taste of Honey, Cesar's, French Connection, Lady Jane, Lady Luck, Lady Strawberry, Mr. Arnold's, Paradise, Pleasure Land, Pleasure Place, Stairway to Heaven, The Sexy Encounter and Venus. Most of the rest came tumbling after.

There are still a couple of strip clubs on the Yonge Street strip, and the odd corporate-style sex toy store, but they abide by strict rules. The rest of the strip is dominated by theaters and more family-oriented shopping.

Prison did not go well for Woods, Kribs and Betesh. They were all sent to Kingston Penitentiary's general population, and saw one another frequently — at least at first.

Woods — whose given name was actually Joseph Michael Woodsworth — applied for parole as soon as he could in 1995. He told the board that he planned to go to New York City to become a dishwasher or sign painter and would seek psychiatric help to "stay normal."

After he denied having anything to do with the murder, attested that he would seek revenge on the Toronto police (who he called "Nazi finks") if released because he said they had made up evidence against him and he had even admitted to slitting Betesh's throat in 1988, it should come as no surprise that he was not freed that time or when he tried again in 1996, 1998 and 2000. Four years were added to Woods' sentence for his assault on Betesh, concurrent with his life sentence.

Woods contracted hepatitis C behind bars, and was transferred to a secure hospital room in Saskatoon where he died of renal failure on April 10, 2003.

Kribs stayed under the radar until his initial parole hearing in 2002. "My feeling is that I should spend the rest of my life in prison," he told them. "As far as I'm concerned, if you do something like that you should never get out. I should die in prison." Since he failed to enroll in a mandatory treatment program for sex offenders, he would have been turned down anyway.

He didn't want to be paroled, but used the hearing as an opportunity to try to set the record straight on a few things. He said that he thought that Emanuel's presence in the apartment was just a cash-for-sex transaction, and had no idea the boy would die. He also said that he didn't drink or do drugs behind bars and had not had sex since he was arrested.

Kribs had been largely unmolested while in the general population at the maximum-security Kingston Pen, but had gotten into numerous fights after being transferred to a medium-security facility. He said it was over personal disagreements, not his status as a sex offender.

He said that he saw Betesh frequently at the Kingston Pen until Woods tried to kill him, and — although they didn't talk — Kribs said he "forgave" him.

Betesh never applied for parole. After he was a, he did give an interview to Toronto Life magazine. "No, I'm not sorry," he told them. "I don't feel anything except sorry that it's put me in here. They say that's part of my illness. I'm not sorry."

After Woods tried to kill him, Betesh was transferred a few miles west to the medium-security Warkworth Institution, which houses many of Canada's convicted sex offenders.

In 2011, Betesh took out an ad on Inmate-Connection.com, an online service that allows prisoners to socialize with people on the outside. Prisoners don't have internet access, so all correspondence is done by mail, although the ad itself is online. In his ad although the ad itself is online, Betesh said he was looking for friends, and wrote:

> "I am 60 years young. I have short hair, blue eyes and
> stands 6 feet tall. I'm slightly overweight but active. I have
> three passions in life 1. Gardening 2. Computers
> (programming not the Internet). 3. Cooking. I am a
> practicing Druid and I also attend Wiccan Services. This is
> the most important part of my life as it concerns my

interaction with the Gods and the planet earth. I will write anyone back who includes a photo.

He did lie, however, when he said he was in prison for "assault."

A year later, Betesh was transferred from Warkworth to the Dorchester Penitentiary in New Brunswick. Corrections Canada doesn't comment on such things, but the Toronto Sun spoke with a prison guard close to the situation under the condition of anonymity. "If taxpayers ever found out how this place runs, the government would have a hard time explaining it" he said. "But we can't say anything or we get fired."

He told the Sun that Betesh had ballooned to 300 pounds behind bars and had become diabetic. Whenever he didn't like something, the guard claimed, Betesh would refuse to take his insulin or go on a hunger strike. Either would send him into a state that required a trip to a civilian hospital under guard, since the prison's medical facilities were unprepared for anything other than first aid.

According to the guard, Betesh had already used the tactic to get a sacred spot, garden and candles to practice his wiccan rituals in, and to have the prison officially recognize his relationship with a fellow prisoner as a civil union.

Since the process of treating Betesh for his frequent insulin shocks had become so labor intensive and expensive, the guard said, Corrections Canada had granted him his wish and Betesh was sent to Dorchester.

The guard also claimed that Betesh had served six months "in the hole" (solitary confinement) after a sexual assault on another prisoner and had also been caught with child pornography.

Chapter 4

Rocky Mountain Madman

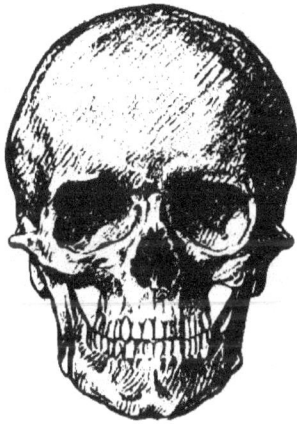

M aureen McKay was tense. Her husband was away at a logging camp, and she had seen a man (or men) creepily hanging around her house in tiny West Creston, B.C. In the interior of British Columbia, she had learned, it wasn't the grizzly bears and mountain lions you had to look out for, it was the men. The logging industry bred and attracted some tough guys, and many had their own inner demons.

So when the phone rang on September 4, 1970, she jumped. She was relieved that it was her cousin, Dale Merle Nelson.

"Do you think you could do without my rifle for a few days?" he asked. "I want to go hunting tomorrow morning." Maureen had borrowed Dale's 7-millimeter Mauser rifle when her husband left for work because of the prowlers in the area. But she knew hunting season opened the next day, and didn't want Dale to miss out, so she agreed. He said he'd come pick it up later that day.

Maureen could tell from his voice that he's been drinking. She wanted to believe her cousin was a good guy, but she knew that he had wrestled with mental illness in the past and had been abusive to the wife and three kids he kept in a tiny shack just outside the woods over in Creston. In fact, he had attempted suicide and been treated at the Riverview Hospital in Coquitlam the previous January. Back then, a visit to Riverview — locally famous as the "loony bin" — was a stigma that could long stick with a person. It didn't help that in June he was convicted of assaulting his wife and sentenced to a year's probation. His rage, it was rumored, came from a long bout of erectile dysfunction.

But Dale, who'd been a lumberjack since he quit school at 16, seemed to Maureen to be getting better. Everybody thought so. Certainly the people he was drinking and strumming guitar with that day at the Kootenay Hotel in Creston didn't notice anything out of the ordinary as he sipped beer after beer and chatted excitedly about hunting season opening. What they didn't know was that as well as the estimated eight to ten beers he had at the hotel, he had also downed another six-pack and a mickey of vodka before coming into the bar.

He then drove his light blue 1966 Chevrolet pickup to Maureen's house. She had invited her next-door neighbor, Shirley Wasyk, over as well. Shirley was Maureen's aunt, but they were all around the same age. In fact, Shirley was actually a year younger than Dale. They had a pleasant conversation in which Shirley mentioned that her husband was out at a work site for a few days, and Dale collected his rifle and left.

He then drove to a nearby gas station, filled up the Chevy and bought a box of bullets. He stopped by to see a friend, Armand Chaleur, had a couple more drinks and then lined up the empty bottles on a fence behind Armand's auto repair shop and shot them all. He ran through his bullets and Armand's booze, so he drove to a sporting goods shop and bought some more ammunition and to a liquor store for some brandy and wine.

It was still light out when he showed up at Creston's King George Hotel and began drinking with his old buddies Rex Smith and John McKay before they headed out to Smith's to continue the party there. After the other guys passed out around midnight, Dale grabbed his gun and took off in his truck.

He ended up at Wasyk's house. She opened the door, invited him in and went into her kitchen to put on some coffee. She knew that Dale could be a handful when he'd been drinking, and he appeared to her to be blind, stinking drunk. With her husband gone and her three daughters in bed, she felt like she needed a little support, so she called Maureen. She happened to have a friend, Frank Chaleur, over and he agreed to go over and see what was going on.

When he got there, Shirley greeted him at the door. To him, she seemed calm and in good spirits. He looked inside the house and saw Dale, who he knew, sitting on the living room couch. Frank asked Shirley if her husband was with them, and she said that he wasn't. Frank would later explain that he got the feeling that the two appeared like they'd rather be alone together, so he left.

With all the commotion, the oldest of Shirley's three daughters, 12-year-old Debbie, had woken up and was listening at her bedroom door trying to find out what was going on. She heard her mother shout "no, Dale, don't!" Curious, she left her bedroom and made it as far as the kitchen, hearing sounds of a struggle from inside her parent's bedroom. When Dale emerged, she hid. She saw him go to her 7-year-old sister Tracy's room and bring her into the kitchen. He hadn't seen Debbie.

Dale then ordered the terrified and shivering Tracy to get him a sharp knife. Debbie watched as Tracy handed the man they called Uncle Dale a 10-inch antler-handled butcher knife. As he led Tracey into the bedroom she shared with 8-year-old Sharlene, Debbie snuck into her parents' bedroom and locked the door behind her.

She saw her mother in bed and rushed to untie her hands, but stopped when she realized that Shirley was dead. When she heard a scream come from her sisters' room, she picked up a bloody fire extinguisher — the weapon that had been used to bash her mom's head in — and threw it through the window. She could hear Dale trying to get into the room as she leapt out the first-floor window and ran.

Debbie made it to Maureen's house and pounded on the door until they let her in. Maureen and Frank were still awake. Moments later, Maureen was screaming into the phone that Dale Nelson had murdered her aunt and was in the process of killing her cousins.

Before she had fled, Dale choked Tracy until she was unconscious, then sliced her from her sternum to below her belly button. He had pulled her stomach and intestines out and cut into them, eating some of the half-digested breakfast cereal he found inside. He also slit her face from ear to ear before leaving her body in her small bed.

Then he grabbed the terrified Sharlene, forced her to perform oral sex, and pulled her toward Shirley's bedroom when he heard the window smash. It was Debbie escaping.

In response to Maureen's call, the RCMP sent Constable Gary McLaughlin. When he saw another car approaching him at extreme speed, he was sure it was the alleged perpetrator trying to escape until the car stopped and its occupants — a man, a woman and a little girl still in her nightgown — flagged him down. It was Maureen, Frank and Debbie. They quickly explained the situation and said that they were taking Debbie to a nearby hospital to treat the wounds she had suffered during her escape.

McLaughlin told Maureen to keep going, but asked Frank to come with him. He radioed for backup, and two more officers — Gus Slomba and Ernie Moker —sped their way to the scene. When McLaughlin and Frank arrived, Frank pointed at the Chevy pickup in the driveway and identified it as Dale's. McLaughlin told Frank to stay behind the police car, and — with his weapon drawn and his eyes on the house's front door, he waited for Slomba and Moker to arrive.

Just after they did, 8-year-old Sharlene came wandering out from behind the house. Moker holstered his gun, ran to the girl, lifted her up and carried her to safety. He then instructed Frank to drive her to the hospital.

Sensing no other life from inside the building, they entered with weapons drawn. The inside of the house was ransacked, with blood, broken glass and debris everywhere. They first came across the body of Shirley, her head caved in, and then that of little Tracy, sliced open like a prize buck.

Dale was nowhere to be seen. Aware that he might go after his own wife and children, McLaughlin and Moker sped back to Creston to evacuate Dale's wife and three children and bring them to a safe house. Slomba went back to the detachment to explain what had happened and get more help.

The three regrouped as soon as they could and went back to the Wasyk house to look for clues. But when they got there, they were stunned to see that Dale's pickup wasn't there anymore. They rushed back into the house with weapons drawn to find that Tracey's body was also no longer there. They had only been gone 15 minutes, but Dale had managed to break back into the house, steal the girl's body and drive away unnoticed. In fact, he had been watching them from the woods the whole time they had been there.

The RCMP detachment was abuzz with the news of the violence in West Creston when a phone rang and silenced everyone inside. Corporal Harvey Finch picked it up and heard a woman scream "There's a man here with a gun!" before the phone clicked and a dial tone took over. He tried calling back several times, but there was no answer. He traced the call to the house of Ray Phipps way out in the woods farther out than the Wasyk place out in West Creston. At 1:30, he and Constable Dennis Schwartz sped to the cabin.

The woman who called was Isabelle St. Amand. For a few years, she and her three kids — Paul, 10, Cathy, 8, and Bryan, 7 — had been living with Phipps, and the couple had their own son, Roy, 18 months earlier.

Finch and Schwartz arrived to see Ray's corpse slumped out the front door. Inside, they found Isabelle, Paul, Bryan and even baby Roy all dead from gunshot wounds. There was no sign of Cathy.

The 10-man RCMP detachment knew they needed help and they called in reinforcements from all over B.C., enlisted some local volunteers and even got the use of a military helicopter to scan the area for any signs of Cathy, Tracey, Dale or his truck. Roadblocks were set up all over the area and a 50-person team with dogs conducted the search on the ground. Little of value was found until mid-afternoon when a pilot who volunteered his floatplane spotted, through the thick fog, a light blue 1966 Chevy pickup in a ditch off an old logging road up in the mountains near Ezekiel Creek.

The police and a few volunteers rushed to the site. The cops approached the truck with their weapons drawn, but Dale was not inside it. Instead, they found that the interior of the pickup was soaked in blood and there was a ball-peen hammer in the passenger seat. It was also stained with blood and had what appeared to be human hair stuck to it. Police and volunteers frantically searched the area. First they found a girl's arm. One searcher later recalled that he hoped it was Tracey's because he held out hope that Cathy was still alive. Then they found Tracy's head, a leg and then the rest of her remains.

After more fruitless scouring of the area, the search was suspended due to darkness.

The following day, more clues were found, including a pair of kid's pajama bottoms and some rope on a tree that investigators determined had been used to tie somebody to it. But it wasn't until RCMP forensics expert Corporal Alan Marcotte went to check on a report that a window in Dale's own house had been removed by someone inside that the case broke open. Marcotte was inspecting the outside of the window when he spotted some footprints heading into the woods. He followed them to find Dale, sound asleep with his head on a log and his rifle within arm's reach.

Rather than confront the suspected killer, Marcotte tiptoed out of the woods and informed the operation's leader, Superintendent Terrance Stewart, of what he had seen. Within minutes, Dale was surrounded by armed officers.

Using bullhorns, they told him that he was surrounded and ordered him to give himself up peacefully. Dale didn't budge, and continued snoring. They repeated the warning. No move from the suspect. They ordered him to give up for a third time, and still he did not respond. Frustrated, the team sent in Constable Glenn Marsden and his dog, Count, to apprehend the suspect. Count's growling woke Dale and the big German shepherd tackled him as he reached for his gun.

The first thing he is reported to have said to them was: "Must have been the LSD."

As soon as he was standing, the cops demanded to know if Cathy St. Amand was still alive. Dale just shook his head. After a few questions, Dale agreed to draw a crude map to show where her body was. Within an hour, they recovered her body, face down and wearing nothing but a T-shirt, in the area he described.

Dale went on trial on March 27, 1971 in nearby Cranbrook for the murders of Tracey and Cathy. The other charges were dropped in an effort to speed his trial.

In it, he recounted the entire story in great detail. After bludgeoning Shirley, he choked Tracey into a state of unconsciousness and sliced her abdomen open while she was still alive. Then he forced Sharlene to perform oral sex. Upon completion he had intended to kill her, but heard a window smash and forced her out the back door and into the woods. As he was dragging her, her feet became entangled in the thick shrubbery and, with the sound of investigators getting closer, he decided to leave her there and escape.

He then recounted how he happened upon the Phipps-St. Amand household at random, killed most of its occupants, abducted Cathy and sodomized her with a wine bottle in the woods while killing her with the hammer after stabbing her in the back.

At his trial, neither side spoke in detail about the LSD. Dale's defense attorney, Michael E. Moran, argued that his actions indicated that he was clearly insane. The Crown, T.G. Bowen-Colthurst, maintained that, while she admitted that Nelson was "crazy," his acts did not fulfil the legal definition of insanity. The jury agreed, and he was found guilty and sentenced to life in prison with no hope for parole for at least ten years.

Dale was never granted parole — prosecutors threatened to put him on trial for the other six murders of he did. He died of complications from throat cancer in the Kent Institution maximum-security prison in Agassiz, B.C., in 1999.

Chapter 5

A Soldier's Story

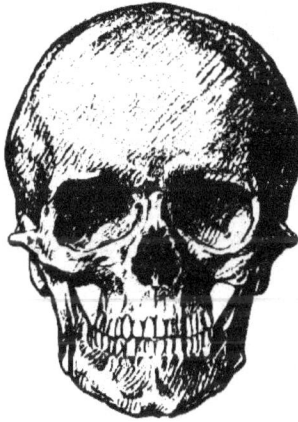

If war is hell, these guys had been there and back. After some of the most intense fighting the Western Allies had seen in the Second World War, the First Canadian Infantry Division, Fifth Canadian Armored Division and the II Polish Corps had managed to break through the Nazi defenses at the world-famous Hitler Line in Central Italy on May 24, 1944.

One of the Canadian soldiers there was Private Harold Joseph "Joe" Pringle.

He and his dad — Joe Senior — traveled from the tiny Eastern Ontario town of Flinton to enlist in 1940, just a few months after the war started. Joe Senior failed his medical examination due to poor eyesight, but his son was accepted and soon on his way to the fighting. Pringle was just 16 at the time, but claimed to be 20. His dad, a 42-year-old veteran of the First World War, backed his story up.

At the time, it was widely believed that a trip to the rough stuff in Central Italy was the reward for being a wayward soldier, and many people wondered why Pringle was still a private almost four years after he enlisted. The fact was that Pringle had been a major disciplinary problem. He had been punished for going AWOL four times, and had even spent six months in a military reformatory camp in England.

He'd been considered a fine soldier in Italy, though, until after the breakthrough when he left his squad mates behind to fight the Nazis while he deserted to Rome.

A few years earlier, in the First World War, the penalty for desertion was death. The Canadian military is known to have executed at least 23 of its own for abandoning their duties in the conflict, and another two were executed for murder. But times had changed, and Canadian soldiers convicted of desertion during the Second World War faced prison, not the noose.

Like most Allied deserters in Italy, Pringle made his way to Rome. Along the way, he ran into an old friend from the stockade, John "Lucky" MacGillivray.

The Eternal City's massive population, the confusion of war and the lack of consistent authority made it easy to hide and survive, even thrive, as a deserter. In fact, Rome had become something of a hotbed of runaway soldiers from many different armies, most of them engaged in gang activity ranging from theft, prostitution and even murder for hire.

Soon after Pringle and MacGillivray arrived in Rome, they fell in with a pair of British deserters — Warrant Officer Bill Croft and Sapper Charlie Honess — who specialized in stealing Allied military equipment and selling it on the black market. Lots of organizations, ranging from fascists to communists, wanted weapons and other materiel, so business was booming. A set of Jeep tires sold for as much as a brand-new car did back home. With more work than they could handle, the gang welcomed Pringle into their little organization. They called it the Sailor Gang because the boss, Croft, had deserted from the Royal Navy and people had started calling him Sailor. Later, two Americans joined the gang.

While the Sailor Gang had been very successful making money, their lack of discipline began to emerge quickly. They would spend whole days blind drunk, and would frequently get into fights, not just with victims and customers, but among themselves.

According to Pringle's testimony, he and Croft were sleeping in an apartment they had chosen to squat in when they heard a gunshot. They both rushed to the apartment across the hall where they knew Honess was staying. What they saw there was MacGillivray laying on his back with blood flowing from a big hole in his gut and a stunned-looking Honess with a pistol in his hand. The pair had been arguing — the reason why lost to history — and Honess had shot the man they called Lucky right in the liver.

MacGillivray was clearly dying. Pringle claimed he begged the other men to take Lucky to a hospital, but they refused. Instead,

Croft and Honess packed the still-alive Cape Bretoner into a stolen Jeep and drove around looking for a secluded spot to dump him.

The eventually came across an out-of-the-way ditch and threw Lucky into it. It's not clear if he was alive or not at that point, but Pringle said that Honess and Croft assured him that he was dead. The gang then decided that it would be smart to fill him full of holes so that it would look like a Mafia assassination.

All of them, including Pringle, shot MacGillivray in the head and chest until he was barely recognizable.

After Allied officials discovered the body, an investigation led to an informant who heard that it was the work of the Sailor Gang or their competitors, the Lane Gang. The members of both organizations were rounded up.

Pringle, sure he was innocent because he believed he only shot Lucky after he was dead, talked. The officers conducting his court martial disagreed, and he was found guilty of murder and sentenced to death. An appeal was quickly denied.

Pringle's original lawyer, Michael Cloney, had an impressive record of acquittals, but was pulled from the case and replaced by a defense attorney who had never tried a case before and was given just a week to prepare. "I can't believe they found him guilty," Cloney told journalist Andrew Clark more than 50 years later. "There was reasonable doubt a mile wide."

It would appear so. The primary witness against Pringle gave four highly inconsistent accounts of what happened, and several forensic experts indicated that it was almost certain that MacGillivray had been dead when Pringle shot him. The only dissenting voice, a British pathologist, later shot himself in the head.

While every civil execution in Canadian history has been by hanging, the military had a different tradition. Early on the morning of July 5, 1945 — less than a month after the German surrender — Pringle was awakened in his holding cell at the Canadian base in Avellino, Italy. Weeks earlier, there had been tens of thousands of Canadians at the base; but, by that morning, there were just 31.

At 7:40 a.m., two military police arrived at his cell. They handcuffed themselves to him and walked him out to a field that had once been a parade ground used by cadets from the youth wing of Mussolini's National Fascist Party. Pringle was then released from the handcuffs. Some sources say he was tied to a post, others say he was seated in a chair that was tied to it. He was given a black hood as a blindfold.

Opposite him were ten soldiers from his own unit. Each was armed with a standard-issue .303-caliber Lee-Enfield bolt-action rifle. Eight were given live rounds, while two were given blanks. At 7:58, after a general read out Pringle's sentence one last time, they fired, killing Pringle instantly.

Sergeant Tony Basciano, a witness, told Clark that Pringle's last words were: "Come on, do what you've got to do. Let's get it over with."

His body was then trucked away and buried in the Canadian section of the Caserta War Cemetery later that day.

In fact, he was buried with full honors and the official record of his death gives no details other than his name, rank, service number, unit and date of death.

That's because his court martial and execution were kept secret and the records of it were sealed for 40 years. There has been no official explanation as to why, but many, including Clark, have pointed an accusing finger at Prime Minister Mackenzie King.

His increasingly unpopular Liberals were facing a federal election on June 20, 1945 — just after the sentence was read and just before it was carried out.

King's supporters and detractors both point to the same reason for secrecy. Honess and Croft had already been executed by the British (the two Americans in the gang were not charged in relation to the murder or the disposal of the corpse), and not doing the same to Pringle for what many saw as essentially the same crime could potentially cause a rift in relations between Canada and Britain, costing the Liberals the election.

Perhaps more important, though, is that King and the Liberals needed to keep Canadians feeling good after the jubilation of Germany's defeat. Knowing about the murder of a Canadian deserter by another Canadian deserter, the quick and questionable trial, the hasty verdict and the cruel sentence would not engender a feeling that we were all still the good guys. Canada had convicted eight other soldiers of murder during the war, and all of them had seen their death sentences commuted to life imprisonment. If the public knew about Pringle's execution, it would look bad for the Liberals.

The Liberals did lose 59 seats, but managed to win a slim majority, returning King to the Prime Minister's office.

It's tempting to say that Pringle was the last Canadian soldier to be executed, but since his death was kept secret for 40 years, it's impossible to know for sure.

Chapter 6

You Don't Know Dick

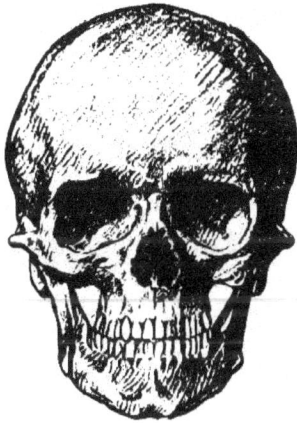

At first, the kids thought they had stumbled upon a dead pig. As they got closer, the recognized that it wasn't a pig at all, but a man. At least part of one.

As was tradition back in the 1940s, Canadian children were ordered out of the house "to play" as soon as they finished breakfast on Saturdays. And these particular kids were especially bored as they tramped around the hill that people in Hamilton call "the Mountain" on the cold morning of March 16, 1946 — until they found the body.

Stunned, the boys ran home to tell their parents. The parents called the cops, who got the kids to show them what they had found.

It was the corpse of a man, but it was missing its head, arms and legs. A couple of bullet wounds were clearly evident. It was obvious to the police that the body had been dumped after a homicide.

At first, the cops thought the killing was linked to organized crime. Hamilton was home to some of North America's most notorious crime figures. The Sicilian and Calabrian Mafia were at the top of the heap, and there were dozens of smaller gangs eager to make a name for themselves. Perhaps, they theorized, the body had been dismembered and left out in the open as a message.

If the killer or killers had attempted to completely remove the cops' ability to identify the corpse, it didn't work. It had a distinctive cyst on one of its buttocks, one that had recently received medical attention, and one undescended testicle. The police canvassed doctors in the area for any man who fit that description.

One quickly emerged. John Dick was born in 1906 to a German family in Molotschna in what was then Russia but is now part of Ukraine. The Dicks emigrated to Canada soon after the Communists took power there in 1917.

John grew up to become a streetcar driver for the Hamilton Street Railway (HSR), and had been reported missing by his cousin Albert Kammerer and his wife, Ann, ten days before the body was found.

Dick was hardly the kind of guy who usually wound up dead in Hamilton. He was deeply religious, a practicing Mennonite, took his job seriously and didn't drink, gamble, visit the city's brothels or take drugs. If it was an organized crime hit, it was probably a case of mistaken identity.

Still, the cops wondered why a guy making pretty decent money without the usual vices would be bunking with his cousin in the city's rough North End.

Kammerer told them that Dick had gotten married six months before, but that it had not been a happy union. He and his wife, Evelyn, fought constantly and when she moved her domineering mother and then her alcoholic father into the house, things got worse. Evelyn soon informed Dick that she would start sharing her bed with her mother instead of him.

Shocked, he said that it was his house and that he made the rules. Alexandra Maclean, his mother-in-law, told him that if he didn't like the new arrangement, he was free to leave. He put his foot down and said that if anyone was going to leave it would be his in-laws or maybe even his wife. But Alexandra reminded him that it was Evelyn who had put down the deposit on the house at 32 Carrick Avenue in Central Hamilton and that the mortgage agreement was in her name. Defeated, Dick took his things and moved in with Kammerer.

While the name Evelyn Dick didn't ring any bells (at least at the time), plenty of the cops knew her by her maiden name, Evelyn Maclean. She was a familiar face on the city's then-active social scene and was reputed to have been involved in many romantic entanglements, most of which included Hamilton's most prominent men.

The Maclean family had been mostly unsuccessful farmers in Beamsville, just outside of Hamilton, when Donald Maclean got a job with the HSR in 1921. He moved his wife, Alexandra, and one-year-old daughter, Evelyn, to a house at 214 Rosslyn Avenue South in the East End of Hamilton.

Their life there was hardly idyllic. Donald — better known as Scotty — was an angry and vindictive man who was also a raging drunk, inveterate gambler and collector of firearms. Alexandra was a stern and domineering Scottish immigrant who had no problem turning the subject of every conversation she had to herself. A former governess at Balmoral Castle (the Royal Family's holiday home in Scotland), she was said to have considered herself in a class above her neighbors and treated them accordingly.

Evelyn was not allowed out to play with the other children, Alexandra claimed, because she was too fragile and weak. Instead, her mother said that she enjoyed cleaning the house to what would now be recognized as an obsessive degree.

As Evelyn got older, she began to sleep in the same bed as her mother, while Donald would pass out either on the living room couch or in the bed in his daughter's room. Later, people close to the case speculated that Alexandra was protecting Evelyn from Donald's sexual advances.

But while Donald was clearly an alcoholic, he certainly was a functioning one. In the early 1930s, he was given a promotion. He went from streetcar driver to accountant at the HSR's downtown headquarters.

Things quickly began to change for the Macleans. Alexandra, who had no job, dressed in furs and sported expensive jewelry, Evelyn was sent to the prestigious Loretto Academy private school for girls downtown and wore the latest fashions. When people inquired about their new-found and much-flaunted wealth, Alexandra explained that a well-to-do aunt back in Scotland had agreed to provide for Evelyn's education and well-being.

But word around town was that Donald was skimming from the tills at the HSR. Back then, there was no way to determine exactly how many riders the system had, so a few bucks either way would be hard to track down. As evidence, Donald's accusers pointed out that he had made major purchases with sacks of nickels and rides on the HSR at the time just happened to be five cents.

After Evelyn left Loretto, Alexandra did her best to transform her into a socialite, which also brought welcome attention to herself. Alexandra bankrolled lavish parties at the city's most luxurious hotel, the Royal Connaught, and invited increasingly important men to celebrate her daughter.

Back in the East End, tongues constantly wagged about Evelyn and her legion of gentleman callers. When she became pregnant in 1942, her mother explained that Evelyn had been married in secret to an American soldier from Cleveland named Norman White, who was stationed in England.

Evelyn gave birth to a daughter, Heather Maria White, on July 10, 1942. A second daughter was stillborn a year and ten days later, and on September 5, 1944, she had a son, Peter David White. Subsequent investigations indicate that Norman White did not exist, and the father or fathers of Evelyn's children were never determined.

Heather was born with a mild intellectual disability, and required significant care from both Evelyn and Alexandra. Neighbors noticed that they stopped seeing and hearing about Peter about two weeks after he was born, to which Alexandra answered that he had been given to the Children's Aid Society for adoption because the family could not afford to keep him.

But still the lavish parties and expensive fashions continued for both her and Evelyn.

Evelyn took Heather to visit Donald at the HSR headquarters and she met John Dick. He was a nice-looking guy and very kind and sincere, a far cry from the gamblers, politicians and Mafiosi she had been accustomed to spending her time with. She turned on the charm and he reciprocated. Impressed by the way he kindly interacted with Heather and delighted that he started to send her gifts, Evelyn agreed to go out with him on a date.

Just a month after their initial meeting, Evelyn agreed to marry him. And six months after that, he was sent to his cousin's house in the North End.

Dick probably didn't know about it, but Alexandra wasn't the only person Evelyn was sleeping with instead of her husband. Within weeks of marrying Dick, Evelyn was out partying. She met Bill

Bohozuk, a strapping and handsome Hamilton steelworker who was also a world-class rower. He took her out to the theater on their first date and she had sex with him afterward.

After the police identified Dick's body, they went to question Evelyn at the Carrick house. She acknowledged that she had heard about the torso that had been found on the Mountain, but her reaction after the cops told her it was her husband shocked even the most hard-bitten among them. "Don't look at me," she said. "I had nothing to do with it."

They took her downtown. Under heavy interrogation, she told them that a flamboyantly dressed Italian man had come to the house looking for John. Evelyn said that she didn't know where he was and asked the man why he wanted to see him. The Italian, she claimed, said that John had slept with another man's wife and that he was going to "fix" — slang at the time for kill — him.

That story struck the detectives as odd. Religious, heart-broken John hardly seemed the type to sleep with another man's wife, let alone a Mafiosi's, and no self-respecting hit man would tell a man's wife, estranged or not, that he was planning a murder, leaving her to testify. They believed Evelyn was playing them for chumps.

While her story didn't hold any water, Evelyn had not incriminated herself. She asked if she could leave. She had every right to, but Hamilton cops, at least back then, were nothing if not crafty and maybe a little willing to bend the rules just a tad. They charged her with vagrancy. In an effort to combat homelessness, the police had the ability to hold anyone who could not produce a house key or enough money to rent a hotel room for the night. Although they had picked Evelyn up at a house that she held the mortgage on, she had left without taking a key or any cash. When she pointed out that she could get both from her house, they told her they couldn't release her because of the vagrancy charge.

They did their best to keep her talking. Eventually, she changed her story. The Italian man hadn't just appeared out of nowhere. She said that Bohozuk had been so overcome by jealousy that he wanted to kill John so that he could marry her himself. She said that

Bohozuk had borrowed $200 in tens and twenties from her so that he could hire a connected guy from Windsor to fix John.

Again, she couldn't convince the cops. Connected guys in Hamilton outnumbered those in Windsor ten to one. You couldn't walk two blocks downtown without running into one. Besides, Mennonite or not, John seemed like he'd be plenty willing to divorce Evelyn and put as much distance between himself and her family as he could.

But they didn't stop her, they just let her keep talking. She changed the story again. In her third version of events, Donald had hired Bohozuk to kill John for reasons unknown.

While she was being questioned, the interrogators learned from a field detective that a man named Bill Landeg reported that Evelyn had borrowed his car a few days before John's body was found and returned the big Packard with blood all over the backseat, bloody clothes in the back seat and a note that apologized for the mess and said that Heather had cut herself. The astute detective had already tested the blood. Its type matched John's and not Heather's.

Evelyn was trapped. She felt she had to admit that she knew John was dead. She changed her story yet again to say that she had received a phone call in which the caller said that John had impregnated another man's wife and that he was "gonna get what's coming to him." The caller then instructed her to get a car and meet him near the Mountain. She did as she was told, she claimed, and when she showed up, the man had a big bloody sack that he said contained pieces of John. Then, under duress, she claimed, she hiked up the mountain with him and helped him toss the remains off a cliff.

Now that she had revealed that she knew that her husband was dead, the police thought that her reaction was hardly appropriate for a widow, even if her marriage was not a successful one. She seemed too calm, like it wasn't a huge deal to be given a bag full of your husband's remains then throw it off a cliff. When they asked her how she felt about her husband's death and dismemberment, she told her questioners that she wasn't happy about it, but that it was a "pretty mean trick to break up a home."

It was at about that time that her lawyer arrived. He got the cops to dismiss the bogus vagrancy claim and let them know that anything she said while being held under it would not be admissible in court.

Later, when questioned with her lawyer present, Evelyn changed her story again. She claimed that Bohozuk and a gang of his friends took John up the mountain, killed and dismembered him and brought her a package of his personal items she might have wanted to keep. Her lawyer pointed out that Bohozuk had been arrested for vagrancy and the possession of an unlicensed handgun less than a week after John's body was found.

When one of the detectives told her that they had already questioned Bohozuk about John's death, Evelyn quickly changed her story again, saying that he had taken her and John up the Mountain in the Packard, shot John and dismembered him in front of her, but that she did not participate.

While she was being held, the police searched both houses. At the Rosslyn residence, they found evidence linked to John, including blood-stained buttons from his HSR uniform, spent cartridges, as well as bone fragments and teeth that had been burned and a bullet hole in a heating duct. They also found $2,000 worth of streetcar tickets. Donald was charged with stealing from his employer.

In the attic of the Carrick house, they found an unusually heavy suitcase. It contained a cement block, inside of which was the body of Peter White, the baby Evelyn had in 1944. He had been wrapped in a skirt with the name E. Maclean sewn into the waistband.

Evelyn was charged with John's murder. Three days later, Bohozuk was also charged with killing John. And then Evelyn and Bohozuk were both charged in connection with Peter's death. Two weeks later, Donald and Alexandra were also charged with John's murder. Charges against Alexandra, however, were soon dropped due to a lack of incriminating evidence.

Evelyn was tried on her own for John's murder beginning on October 7, 1946. Although there was no actual physical evidence to link her to the crime, the prosecution argued that her "wickedness" (especially her admitted promiscuity) and her own statements were enough to convict her. Nine days later, after two hours of deliberation, the jury found her guilty, but recommended leniency. The judge disagreed, sentencing her to death. She was scheduled to be hanged on January 7, 1947.

From jail, Evelyn hired star lawyer J.J. Robinette, who had taken an interest in the case. He argued at her appeal hearing that the statements used against her in the first trial were inadmissible because she had made them while charged with vagrancy, not murder, she had not been warned that they would be used against her and that she was not told that she could remain silent until her lawyer arrived. All five justices agreed that she deserved a new trial.

She was tried alone again, beginning February 24, 1947. This time, her statements to police were not included. Robinette argued that all the evidence the prosecution had presented pointed to Donald as John's killer, not Evelyn. He did admit that it was very likely that Evelyn had served as an accessory after the fact, but that she had not been charged as such. She was on trial for John's murder, and there was no compelling evidence that she had killed him. Robinette went so far as to say that no jury in the land would "hang a dog" based on the Crown's evidence. She was acquitted on March 6.

Her third trial, that for the murder of Peter White, began on March 24. Again represented by Robinette, her defense was that all of the evidence against her was entirely circumstantial — anybody could have asphyxiated the boy and wrapped him in her skirt. Even if she had killed him, she was suffering from the stress of raising a special-needs child as a single mother with abusive parents at the time. The jury returned a guilty verdict, but not for murder, but manslaughter. The Crown appealed, unsuccessfully.

At her sentencing, psychiatrist Robert Finlayson testified that Evelyn had an IQ in the low 80s, which he said put her between categories her called "dull normal" and "moron-like." He went on to declare that she had the "mental age" of 12 or 13, indicating she was incapable of mature thought and decision-making. Still, the judge slapped her with life in prison, the maximum sentence he was allowed to administer.

Two days later, the joint murder trial of Bohozuk and Donald began. Because the only evidence against Bohozuk were statements by Evelyn and they had been made inadmissible and she refused to make any new ones, he walked. Facing a mountain of physical evidence, Donald plea bargained to the lesser charge of being an accessory after the fact, and was sentenced to five years in prison.

Donald served his time and died a few years later. Alexandra died in 1964 and Bohozuk hung on until 1996.

Evelyn was released from Kingston's Prison for Women in 1958, after serving 11 years. At her parole hearing, chairman and director of the John Howard Society J. Alex Edmison argued that her name was so well known by Canadians that she should be granted a new identity. Under an assumed name, Evelyn Dick then did her best to disappear from history.

Journalists and private detectives tried tirelessly to track her down. There were frequent reports of Evelyn sightings, mainly in London and Kitchener, for years. But her biographer, Brian Vallée, determined that she had moved to Western Canada and married again. He also discovered that Heather had changed her last name and was married with a daughter in Toronto.

The trials were sensations. Every time Evelyn arrived at the Wentworth County courthouse, she was greeted by throngs of curiosity-seekers and mobs of protesters throwing eggs and screaming "whore," "slut" and "harlot." The media unfailingly referred to her as "pretty" and "comely," and reported on her outfits as though she was a runway model at an haute couture show.

At the time, Hamilton children came up with a somewhat ribald schoolyard chant about her:

You cut off his legs ...
You cut off his arms ...
You cut off his head ...
How could you, Mrs. Dick?
How could you, Mrs. Dick?

Her story has been immortalized in several books, songs, a musical and even a 2002 made-for-TV movie. People still visit the Carrick and especially Rosslynn house to take photos. And in every one of telling of the torso story, Evelyn is portrayed as a cool and calculating criminal, climbing her way up social circles and meticulously plotting the diabolical murder of her husband.

While that can make for some exciting drama, it's historically inaccurate. The truth appears to be a lot more mundane and, frankly, more than a little pathetic.

Evelyn was a woman with significant mental limitations and emotional problems who was abused by both of her parents, exploited sexually by the city's connected men so that her mother could bask in social elevation and blamed for the murder and grisly disposal of her estranged husband.

The police took advantage of her guilelessness and coerced statements out of her with a charge of vagrancy they knew was false. Although those statements were not legally admissible, they were enough to get a court to sentence her to death.

The Canadian government was prepared to hang a developmentally disabled woman on evidence that was illegally obtained, and still circumstantial. It was only the intervention of the nation's best-known lawyer that saved her life.

In all likelihood, John was killed by Donald in the basement of the Rosslyn house because he found out that his father-in-law was stealing from their shared employer and, perhaps, threatened to tell on him. And the tired old alcoholic just did a poor job of disposing the body, ineffectively attempting to incinerate some of it in the house's furnace before finally dumping the rest over a small cliff a few hundred feet from the scene of the crime.

Evelyn might have helped dispose of the body, but was never charged with it. She was convicted of infanticide, an act that has not resulted in a sentence of more than a year since the 1960s and one that some Canadians argue should be stricken from the Criminal Code altogether. Evelyn was sentenced to life, but was paroled after 11 years. She did her time, and then did her best to vanish. Instead, she became a legend.

Chapter 7

Mobster Princess

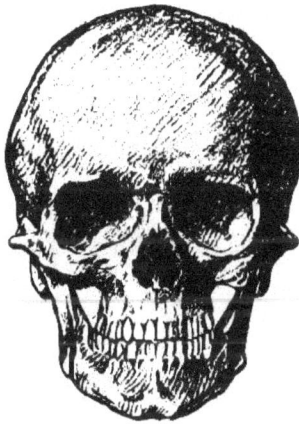

Florence Lassandro must've thought there were some pretty strange people in Canada. All her life, from Italy to Alberta to Pennsylvania to B.C. and back to Alberta, everybody she knew liked to drink. The Holy Roman Catholic Church even insisted upon it (the Blessed Sacrament might magically turn into Christ's blood, but it sure tastes a lot like wine). But for some reason, first Alberta, then B.C., then pretty well everywhere else banned the sale of alcohol except for "scientific, medical or sacred use."

Not that she minded. Prohibition allowed her and her husband, her husband, Charles Lassandro, to make a good living — and they were never without wine. That's because they both worked at the Alberta Hotel in Blairmore, Alberta, for a man the locals all called Emperor Pic and they knew as Emilio.

Emilio Picariello was born in Sicily sometime in the late 1870s. At the time, many Sicilians were extremely resentful of the Italian takeover of their island, and after martial law had been declared there, huge numbers of them emigrated, mostly to the U.S. and Canada. In 1899, young Emilio left the island and by 1902, he had made his way to Toronto.

There were not a lot of jobs open to Sicilian immigrants in Canada at the time. They could forget factory or farm work, mining or anything that required good English skills. Instead, they were laborers, often involved in paving, masonry, restaurant work or trash removal. Emilio worked as a laborer and lived in a boarding house, saving his money. He married the boarding house's young housekeeper, Maria Marucci, and bought a grocery store where he stocked items catering to an increasingly large Sicilian population. Emilio and Maria contributed to that particular baby boom with seven kids of their own.

In 1911, he heard from Giuseppe Maranino. His old friend from Sicily had struck it rich when he opened a macaroni factory in the mining boom town of Fernie, B.C. He invited Emilio to come work for him. It didn't take Emilio long to decide. Toronto was crowded and dirty. The people outside of the Sicilian community weren't happy about their presence and some of the people inside the community were beginning to lean pretty heavily on shop owners like him, demanding protection payments and taking whatever they wanted without paying.

Emilio worked for Maranino for a few years and bought the factory from him when he went chasing another boom in Lethbridge, Alberta.

Emilio saw no future in macaroni, and started employing local women to make high-quality cigars. It was an immediate success. As he got wealthier, he diversified into peddling other pleasures. He started selling wine and, in the summer, he made ice cream, which he sold throughout the region on a wagon.

The wine company he sold for always needed bottles, so he often accepted bottles in exchange for ice cream. The trade became so lucrative for him that he cornered the Crowsnest Pass bottle market and became known as the Bottle King. He even used that title in newspaper advertisements, one of which read: "E. Picariello, the Bottle King, requests that all persons selling bottles hold them until they see E. Picariello, who pays top prices."

As he became wealthier and more prominent, he became more diplomatic. He went by Emil among his non-Sicilian friends and customers and groomed a friendly, avuncular image for himself.

It was important for him to be seen as one of the guys because Fernie was a town fraught with ethnic unrest. The First World War was raging and the daily reports of horrifying numbers of young men dying dominated the news and conversations of the day. Arguments and fights broke out in the mines, and by 1915, miners of English and Scottish descent walked off the job. They refused to go back to work until men from enemy states — Germany, the Austro-Hungarian Empire and the Ottoman Empire — were interned.

With the blessing of B.C. Premier Richard McBride, local authorities rounded up all unmarried men from the enemy states or married ones whose wives still lived overseas and held them as prisoners of war until the end of hostilities.

Emilio lucked out when Italy switched sides early and declared war on the British Empire's enemies. Still, he made a big show of his patriotism, investing $5,000 in war bonds and providing financial aid to striking miners.

While war was raging, several groups — mainly Protestant clergy — campaigned for alcohol prohibition. And Alberta, in 1916, was the fourth jurisdiction in Canada to pass a law banning the sale of alcohol. But the Alberta law was full of loopholes. Alcohol could be used medicinally, and pharmacies got rich selling 40-ounce doses of beer. Beer with less than 2.5 percent alcohol was legal, and it was up to the honesty of the labelers to maintain that rule. And, most important, Albertans could buy limited amounts of alcohol for private, in-home consumption from other Canadian provinces.

It was the perfect opportunity for the bottle king. Already Fernie's biggest supplier of wine, he started moving all kinds of alcohol to customers in Alberta through Crowsnest Pass.

It was immensely popular, and soon dwarfed his other businesses in revenue. It was so successful, in fact, that he bought three brand-new Ford Model Ts and hired a full-time mechanic. At first, it was all legal, but Emilio couldn't resist making a few extra bucks by exceeding the limits, and started to employ bootlegger's tricks to get around them.

The glory days lasted until B.C. enacted its own prohibition law a little more than a year later. And then times got better.

Faced with a huge number of thirsty customers in Alberta and no legal supply, Emilio decided that the profits in alcohol importation were too high for him to maintain a law-abiding lifestyle. He packed up his operation in Fernie and moved it to Blairmore, Alberta, on the flat side of Crowsnest Pass. More important, Blairmore had something Fernie did not at the time — a direct route to the U.S. Prohibition had not yet been enacted south of the border, and liquor was freely available in Montana.

Importing it into Canada, however, was strictly illegal. At first, the road was rarely patrolled, but as word got out, the Alberta Provincial Police — an organization that was formed in a large part to enforce prohibition because of the NWMP's reluctance to do so — began to crack down. They set up roadblocks, which Emilio fought at first through trickery — hiding alcohol under flour sacks or sending an empty bait car through the roadblock and sneaking another one past after the cops left — and then through outspending. He replaced the three Model Ts with six McLaughlin-Buick Light 6s, which could easily outrun the APP's cars if necessary. In fact, the cars were so associated with bootleggers, they were known as Whisky 6s by many.

He bought the Alberta Hotel, not just as a legitimate business front, but because he needed the space. He excavated the building's basement to serve as a liquor warehouse, and built a tunnel down to it that opened into a private alley.

Politicians changed things for Emilio again. In the fall of 1919, the United States ratified the Volstead Act, its own nation-wide prohibition law, despite President Woodrow Wilson's veto. Just as Emilio's stocks from Montana were drying out, B.C. repealed their anti-alcohol laws. Without missing a beat, he abandoned his routes in from Montana and re-established his pipeline from Fernie.

That's not to say he didn't get caught from time to time. In 1921, APP officers found some empty beer barrels in his ice cream warehouse. Emilio gladly paid his $20 fine. A few months later, police in Montana searched a rail car and found 70 beer barrels that were addressed to Emilio in Alberta. He fought that case, claiming he had bought soda water and that his supplier mixed up the order, but was found guilty and fined $500.

Convicted bootlegger or not, the rich, generous and eminently affable Emilio was very popular in Blairmore, and was elected alderman. He even donated the flour he used to hide his booze to poor families in the area.

Those were heady days for the former laborer. He had wealth, respect, political office and he was not just the region's biggest supplier of ice cream and booze, but one of its biggest employers.

One of his most trusted employees was a fellow Sicilian named
Charles Lassandro. Well, he wasn't exactly named Charles
Lassandro. He was born Carlo Sanfidele, and changed his first name
to Charles after he immigrated to Canada, and his family name to
Lassandro after he compiled some life-threateningly large gambling
debts when he lived in the Pittsburgh area for a short time.

Charles wasn't very good at anything legal, but Emilio kept him
around because he was an old friend and because he was pretty
useful in the bootlegging business.

Emilio also employed Charles' wife, Florence. Born Philumena
(some sources say Filumena) Costanzo in Sicily in 1900, she came to
Canada with her family in 1909. Almost immediately, a teacher
insisted she change her name to Florence. Her parents complied and
in 1915, set her up in an arranged marriage to Charlie. Emilio hosted
the event and served as best man. Rumors at the time claimed that
it was a Sicilian tradition for the best man to sleep with the pretty
14-year-old bride and that Emilio took on the task with vigor, but it
has no historical basis.

Charles and Florence did not have a particularly happy marriage,
and she did not appreciate being taken from Fernie to Pittsburgh,
back to Fernie and then to Blairmore and going from being a
Costanzo to a Sanfidele to a Lassandro. But she did enjoy Emilio's
company and the fact that he respected her enough to give her
important jobs in all of his businesses, including bootlegging. She
was also widely reputed to have been enjoying a romance at the time
with Emilio's handsome son Steve (born Stefano).

Although she began her career at the Alberta Hotel as a waitress,
Florence soon graduated to more important duties. Because she was
so presentable and polite, she would often accompany Steve in the
decoy car, posing as the young couple many said they were. Florence
took to it quickly and would sometimes make runs on her own. She
was known as something of a daredevil and had a reputation for
driving at speeds most people considered dangerous.

It was a routine run from Fernie on September 21, 1922 with
three cars — one with Emilio's mechanic, J.J. McAlpine, another
with Steve and with Emilio himself at the wheel of the third — when

everything began to fall apart. The APP detachment in Blairmore received a tip that Emilio and his crew would be bringing an illegal load in that day.

They quickly alerted the detachment in Coleman, on the B.C.-Alberta border. One of their officers — Constable Stephen Longacres Lawson, who knew the Picariello family from when he was part of the Fernie police force — kept an eye on the road, and when he saw the three McLaughlins roll past, he radioed the cops in Blairmore. They quickly got a search warrant for the cars and the hotel. They then waited for the convoy in front of the Alberta Hotel.

When the bootleggers arrived, Emilio, his car by then in front, could tell something was up. There were a couple of armed, uniformed cops in front of his place. When they presented him with the search warrant, he honked his horn in a sequence that was a pre-arranged warning. That triggered Steve, who turned his McLaughlin around and sped back to B.C. Then Emilio reversed while turning and drove back onto the road, blocking the cops' own car, preventing them from chasing Steve.

The cops then ran back to the detachment to radio Lawson in Coleman. Emilio took the opportunity to follow his son back to Fernie so he could sort things out.

It wasn't long before Steve's big McLaughlin went roaring through Coleman. Lawson was waiting. He shouted at Steve to stop, then fired a warning shot in the air. Steve kept his foot on the accelerator and nearly hit Lawson. His warnings unheeded, Lawson took another shot — this time directly at the car — as it zoomed by. He then flagged down the next car that came down the road, told the driver he needed to commandeer the vehicle, and took off after Steve. A flat tire forced him to watch as the suspect drove out of his jurisdiction.

Not long after, Emilio's car came roaring into sight. Gun out, Lawson flagged him down. The cop told the Bottle King he knew what was up and that Emilio had better bring his son back to Alberta, or the cops would. Emilio was noncommittal, and returned to Blairmore.

When he got there, the cops were searching the hotel. He quickly recognized Sergeant James Scott, head of the APP's Blairmore detachment, and told him he wasn't going to find anything. Angered, Scott told Emilio that he'd charge him and his son with dangerous driving. Emilio laughed and said he didn't care about some petty fine because his cargo was sitting waiting for him in B.C. and it was worth a lot more than any fines Scott could throw at him.

Emboldened, he told Scott that Lawson was lucky he hadn't hit Steve when he shot at him, or he'd take care of him himself. Scott then told him that Steve had been hit — there was blood at the site of the shooting — but because he had fled into B.C., they didn't know how badly he was injured.

Suddenly silent, Emilio went home, put two guns under his overcoat and grabbed Florence.

Again, he sped his way to Coleman. He found the police barracks and called Lawson out. At first, the two men had a heated, but civil, conversation in which Emilio asked Lawson what happened and asked him if he could help his son. But as the two began to argue, it got physical. Although there are several different popular versions of what happened next, the most frequently told story is that the two separated and that when Lawson turned to return home, he was shot in the back.

At that point, Emilio panicked and fled. He went back to Blairmore, but knew that he and his car would be instantly recognized anywhere near the hotel, so — under cover of darkness — he and Florence found an abandoned shack near the edge of town and spent the night. When they woke up the following morning, Emilio told Florence she was on her own and ran into the wooded hills east of town.

After an alert for was issued to police all over the area, he was arrested the next day by the APP. He immediately asked them how his son was doing. The cops told him that Steve had been shot in his left hand, and should heal soon. Emilio seemed relieved, but when they also told him that Lawson was dead and that his 9-year-old daughter, Pearl, had witnessed the killing, Emilio appeared emotionless.

Florence turned herself in the next day, and both were charged with Lawson's murder. Steve, who spent the night in an unoccupied house in the since-abandoned town of Michel, B.C., surrendered to police in Fernie in search of medical attention. He was not charged.

Local interest in the case was so great, that its preliminary hearing had to be relocated to the 500-seat Coleman Opera House. Still, people were turned away. Sensing that the people of the Crowsnest Pass region were too invested in the case, chief defense counsel J. McKinley Cameron requested a relocation. It was granted, and the pair were to be tried in Calgary.

The actual trial was a messy and inconsistent affair. Cameron first tried to argue that nobody actually saw who fired the shot (the witnesses were watching Lawson at the time), so it could have been anyone. When that didn't fly, he tried to convince the jury that Emilio had fired out of self-defense, fearing that Lawson was headed inside to get a weapon. When it appeared that the case was going bad for Emilio, Florence admitted that she had shot Lawson.

Many speculated at the time that she was taking the blame for her boss because he would almost certainly face the death penalty if convicted, and she would not. Canada had lost its taste for executing women, and hadn't done so since 1899. One Quebec woman, Marie-Anne Gagnon, had been sentenced to hang in Quebec City because of the heinousness of her torturing her 10-year-old stepdaughter to death, but she was granted clemency when she gave birth to twins while incarcerated. No woman had ever been hanged in Alberta.

If Florence's confession was a ploy to save Emilio, it didn't work. After the judge, William Legh Walsh, told the jury it didn't matter which of the defendants actually shot Lawson and that they could find them both guilty if they chose, they returned a guilty verdict for both. Both were sentenced to hang. "The only thing that can be said in favor of the prisoner, Lassandro, is that she is a woman," Walsh told the court. "I know, of course, quite well the reluctance that there is to execute the death sentence upon a woman and that, of late years at any rate, such a thing has not been done in

Canada. That is, of course, a question of principle which is not for me. If she was a man, there could be no question but that the sentence should be executed."

As news of the sentence spread through Canada, a grassroots movement to commute her sentence grew. Newspaper editorials (which often called her a "Mobster Princess") begged for clemency, demonstrations on her behalf were held and stacks and stacks of petitions reached the prime minister's desk. Many pointed out that Florence had indeed recanted her confession, admitting that she thought she could save Emilio from the noose by taking the rap. "We agreed that it would be best for me to take the responsibility and say that I did it, as women don't hang in Canada and he would get off," Florence wrote in a telegram to Minister of Justice Sir Jean Lomer Gouin. "I am positive that I never had a gun in my hands. I never shot a gun in my life — was always afraid of them."

There were opponents to clemency, mainly men who tut-tutted that chivalry was dead. But one person who wanted to see Florence hang was different, and people listened to her. Emily Murphy was an outspoken and charismatic feminist who also happened to be a judge. She would later become world famous in 1927 when she managed to get the British Crown to overturn a Canadian Supreme Court decision that women were not "persons" under Canadian law.

In a letter to Prime Minister William Lyon Mackenzie King, she wrote: "As women, we claim the privilege of citizenship for our sex, and accordingly are prepared to take upon ourselves the weight of these penalties as well." She pointed out that the death penalty is intended as the ultimate deterrence, and if Florence did not hang, it would be a clear message to all murderers that they should find a woman to take the fall for them.

On the morning of May 2, 1923. Emilio ate a hearty breakfast at the Fort Saskatchewan jail and then was escorted to the gallows. He told the executioner that he did not want the customary hood because he wanted to see what was coming to him. He then told the assembled officials: "You are hanging an innocent man; God help me."

After his body was taken away, Florence was led to the same platform. Adjustments were made to accommodate her small size. Unlike her boss, she hadn't eaten anything. She hadn't slept either, dedicating her last night on Earth to prayer. "Why do you hang me when I didn't do anything?" she shouted at the crowd. "Is there not anyone who has any pity?" The response was silence. Her last words were "I forgive everybody."

Her family sent a request asking that her remains be returned to Blairmore, but it was refused and both Emilio and Florence were buried in unmarked graves in Edmonton.

Alberta never executed another woman, and repealed its prohibition laws a little more than a year later.

Chapter 8

Canadian Nazis

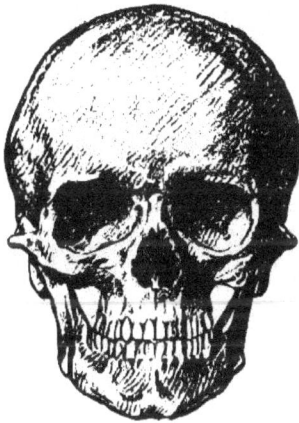

Julius Streicher was not just a Nazi, but he was a Nazi whose anti-Semitic rhetoric was too strident even for other Nazis. After fighting in the First World War, Streicher became convinced that Germany's loss and subsequent agreement to humiliating terms from the Allies were caused by Bolsheviks and Jews. In 1921, he heard Adolf Hitler speak at a rally, which solidified his opinions. Streicher said he was "transformed" by the experience, and he and some of his like-minded friends joined the fledgling Nazi Party, doubling its membership.

When Hitler came to power, Streicher was rewarded for his loyalty. The Nazi party bankrolled his anti-Semitic newspaper, Der Stürmer (The Striker), and three children's books, in which the villains were always Jews. He was also made gauleiter, a post similar to a governor, of Franconia, part of Bavaria.

Although he continued to be friends with Hitler, Streicher's strident anti-Semitism was too much for most of the Nazi establishment, and he was eased from power in 1940, although he was still allowed to continue to publish Der Stürmer.

After the war, Streicher was captured by the Americans and put on trial at Nuremberg. Found guilty of crimes against humanity, he was sentenced to death. He and nine other prominent Nazis were brought to a multi-noose gallows on October 16, 1946. While the others were silent, Streicher shouted "Heil Hitler!" as he was brought in, reputedly spat on his hangman and then screamed "The Bolsheviks will hang you!" as the noose was placed over his neck.

While much of the world was happy to see the end of Julius Streicher, at least one family mourned him deeply. The Dröges of Forchheim in Upper Franconia would miss "Uncle Julius" dearly.

On September 25, 1949, almost three years after Streicher was executed, Wolfgang Dröge was born. His grandfather, one of Streicher's best friends and a former member of the Nazi Party, and his father, a Luftwaffe pilot who had been injured in the war, told little Wolfgang all about how great their famous family friend was and told him stories about how one day an all-white nation, with no Jews and no Bolsheviks, would arise, and it would be like paradise on Earth.

As Wolfgang got older, things changed. Most Germans distanced themselves from their Nazi past and worried more about the possibility of a nuclear war fought between the United States and its allies against the Soviet Union and its allies in their own homeland.

And Wolfgang's parents' marriage began to break up. His father threatened his mother with violence to the point at which she said she feared for her life.

Finally, in 1962, with Wolfgang just 12 years old, she emigrated to Canada with her son. As was the custom of the time, Wolfgang's mother changed her surname to Droege, because Canadian typewriters of the time couldn't handle umlauts.

In 1967, Wolfgang returned to West Germany to join its army. He was refused. He told family and friends that they turned him down because he was too young, but that doesn't ring true. The age of enlistment for the army is 18, and — although Wolfgang arrived in Germany before his eighteenth birthday — he stayed in the country well past he the point when he became of age and did not make a second attempt.

While in Germany, he hooked up with a few other like-minded people, and started attending neo-Nazi meetings. He had long suspected such things existed, but had been unable to find any in Canada. The friends he made in West Germany, however, had several contacts in Canada and the United States, and passed their information onto Wolfgang.

He returned to Canada, working at various jobs in places like Sudbury before settling down to become a printer in Toronto.

In 1974, he met and befriended Don Andrews. Although Nazis had killed his father and had separated him from his mother and forced her to work in a slave labor camp, Don — born Vilim Zlomislić in Croatia in 1942 — became one of them.

When the war was over, his mother, told that he had been killed in an air raid, married Canadian soldier Frederick Andrews and moved to Toronto.

Vilim lived in a Yugoslavian orphanage, and was pressed into service for the communist Young Pioneers. On a camping trip, he severely injured his leg. He believed that the surgeons who worked on him botched his operation — leaving him with terrible scars and a life-long limp — because communism had robbed them of their ambition to do a decent job.

Through the help of the Red Cross, Vilim's mother found him in 1952, and he was brought to Canada and renamed Donald Clarke Andrews.

In 1967, Andrews and friends Paul Fromm, Al Overfield and Leigh Smith formed a group they called the Edmund Burke Society, borrowing the name from some more benign debate clubs at U.S. colleges.

The Edmund Burke Society advertised itself as being an anti-communist, anti-elitist group supporting traditional values. But it was in fact a front for white supremacists, who disrupted any event they saw as promoting communism or the mixing of races.

The Edmund Burke Society rose to national prominence when controversial American civil rights lawyer William Kunstler spoke at the University of Toronto in 1970. Fromm burst from the crowd and poured a glass of water on Kunstler's notes. That prompted Kunstler to pour an entire pitcher of water on Fromm's head. The crowd went wild, and Fromm was knocked unconscious in the ensuing melee.

The following year, against the wishes of his security detail, Prime Minister Pierre Trudeau invited Soviet Premier Alexei Kosygin to walk around the streets of Ottawa with him. Geza Matrai — an Edmund Burke Society member, wrestler and hairdresser — saw them and felt compelled to act. While shouting "Vive Free

Hungary!" he leapt onto Kosygin's back, wrestling him almost to the ground. He was dragged off and spent two months in jail.

Several members of the Edmund Burke Society, perhaps in hopes of gaining some mainstream credibility, formed what they called the Social Credit Party of Ontario and ran in elections under the SoCred banner even though the national Social Credit party disavowed any connection to them.

Internal disagreements in policy tore at the Edmund Burke Society, and by the end of 1972, it ceased to exist.

Andrews and Fromm weren't done as activists yet, though, and formed the Western Guard (later the Western Guard Party). Unlike the Edmund Burke Society, the Western Guard had no veneer of mainstream politesse. It was openly dedicated to racial segregation and anti-Semitism.

Fromm left the party as Andrews increasingly focused on violent methods of protest, and it was at about that time that Wolfgang showed up as an ambitious young recruit.

Droege quickly earned his stripes. On the night before a march for African Liberation Day in 1975, he spray-painted the words "white power" on several locations along the route. He was found, charged, convicted and spent a few days in jail.

Not long after, he attended the 1976 International Patriotic Congress in Metairie, Louisiana. One of the speakers was David Duke, Imperial Wizard of the Ku Klux Klan. Wolfgang was so impressed that he formed a KKK chapter in Toronto and laid the foundation for another in British Columbia. While Wolfgang founded the Canadian KKK, its official president was his friend James McQuirter who was described as better looking and more polished on camera.

After a plot to bomb the Israeli soccer team was uncovered, Andrews went to jail and the Western Guard began to lose members under the sometimes-bizarre leadership of John Ross Taylor.

One of them was Wolfgang, who quickly joined the Nationalist Party of Canada, which Andrews had formed upon his release in 1978.

Wolfgang remained in contact with Duke — even convincing him to come to Toronto to stir up publicity — and in 1979, Duke introduced him to fellow Klansman Mike Perdue. Perdue had a plan to violently overthrow the government of the island of Grenada to set up drug trafficking and other businesses there to supply funds for the KKK. Wolfgang was interested, and it was decided that he would be the plan's primary fundraiser.

Andrews was also part of the plan, but he withdrew after Perdue changed the target nation from Grenada to Dominica — a much smaller nation that was, at the time, beset by a hurricane-cased financial crisis, gang violence and had only a token military.

While Wolfgang was raising money, the first person he hit up was London, Ontario's Martin K. Weiche. Weiche — whose son David was a member of the ill-fated Bandidos motorcycle gang — later denied contributing, but admitted that he was part of the plan. He said that he had been sold on the idea not of moving drugs, but of creating a colony for "all pure whites — Aryan stock, physically as well as mentally."

The plan unraveled pretty quickly. In February 1981, the captain of the boat they intended to use backed out, and they had to look for another. They settled on Michael S. Howell, a Vietnam combat veteran, and well-known New Orleans boat captain. He initially agreed to take the group to Dominica, but when he found out that his clients would be carrying guns and explosives, he changed his mind. Desperate, Perdue told him that his team were carrying out a covert mission for the CIA. Howell was suspicious, but said that he would take them.

As soon as Perdue left, Howell called the ATF and told them what he knew. That started a chain reaction that resulted in the arrest of Patrick John — a former prime minister of Dominica the collaborators had agreed to bring back to power if he would allow them to operate unmolested on the island — on April 25, 1981.

Even though they had heard about John's arrest in Dominica, the conspirators decided to go ahead with their plan anyway and, on April 27, they drove to the marina Howell's boat was in.

When they arrived, they were met by dozens of heavily armed FBI, ATF and Customs officers. Blinded by spotlights and down the barrels of automatic weapons, the would-be army gave up on the spot. Authorities seized several automatic weapons, shotguns, rifles, handguns, dynamite, more than 5,000 rounds of ammunition and a Nazi flag.

Eight Americans and six Canadians — Wolfgang, McQuirter, Larry Lloyd Jacklin, Marion McGuire, Charles Yanover and Harold Woods — were arrested.

McQuirter was not part of the original bust. In a moment of unrestrained hubris, he called a reporter at CFTR news radio and told him of his involvement in an effort to gain more publicity for the far right locally. The reporter called the OPP and McQuirter was charged with conspiracy to overthrow a foreign government and fraud. The investigation into his involvement in the failed coup attempt also uncovered a plot he had to kill his wife's previous boyfriend.

Wolfgang was sentenced to three years, McQuirter to two for the coup plot and five more for the murder plot.

With Wolfgang and McQuirter in prison, leadership of the Canadian KKK fell to Wolfgang's girlfriend, a woman the media calls Ann Farmer, who moved its base of operations to suburban Vancouver.

Years later, Wolfgang would look back at the coup attempt fondly. "We had the men and the resources," he told a reporter. "It was just unfortunate that we got caught."

He also said that going to prison helped him get ahead as a white supremacist. "Jail wasn't that bad," he said. "It really put American society and the racial issue into perspective. Plus, it gave me an opportunity to network with other racialist leaders, which really helped me after I got out."

While he was in prison, Wolfgang received encouraging letters from influential white supremacist leaders like Duke, Tom Metzger of the White Aryan Resistance and Robert Miles of the Aryan Nations.

Upon his release, Wolfgang was supposed to go back to Canada, but instead chose to stay in Huntsville, Alabama. Unable to get a legitimate job, he dealt in stolen goods, including vehicles, and cocaine.

In November 1984, he was arrested while trying to board an airplane with an illegal knife. A search of his bags uncovered a large amount of cocaine. He was sentenced to 13 years in a federal penitentiary.

He was sent to USP Lompoc in California. A racially diverse prison, the white gangs (including Aryan Nations) there are quite powerful because they have a strong handle on the internal drug trade.

Released in April 1989, Wolfgang returned to Toronto where he was heartily welcomed by Andrews and his other white supremacist friends. Wolfgang was penniless, and he was helped with cash, food and accommodation by other members of the Nationalist Party.

According to an undercover agent who was embedded in the party's hierarchy, Wolfgang had intended to move to B.C. to be with Farmer, but was convinced to stay in the Toronto area to start a group he called Society for the Preservation of the White Race. He later changed the name to the White Heritage Foundation, and described it as "a group of dedicated white nationalists whose interest it would be to force the government to include their mandate in the government agenda. The White Heritage Foundation would also act as a lobby group to protect the rights of white people."

Wolfgang admitted that that was just the public side of the White Heritage Foundation, and that it would also engage in covert activities in an effort to establish and maintain an all-white enclave in Ontario, using "whatever persuasive methods or inducements necessary to convince non-whites to leave the area."

To make a living, he was given a job as a private bailiff — in Ontario, basically a repo man — at Overfield's company.

Not long after, Andrews told his group that he would require some of them to fly to Libya to take part in the Twentieth Anniversary Celebration of the Libyan Revolution. The tickets were bought and paid for (he hinted that it was by the Libyan government), although the participants would have to pay for their own accommodation during an overnight stopover in Rome.

Seventeen people, including Wolfgang, agreed to go. Andrews begged out, saying that a pending court appearance prevented him from leaving the province.

The flight to Rome was fine, but things fell apart once they got there. At the airport, Italian officials separated four members of the group, including Wolfgang, for questioning.

The Italians didn't really have any reason to hold them, they were just trying to intimidate them. One of the officers said to the group "you don't want to go to Libya, it's too hot."

One of the Nationalists, Max French, remarked "we'll wear shorts," and Wolfgang told him to shut up.

The plane did not fly them to Libya, but only to the island of Malta, about halfway to Libya's capital, Tripoli. The white supremacists then had to share a ship they called a "converted prison ship" with many Africans who they took great pains to avoid.

Once in Libya, they were accommodated at an outdoor camp away from Tripoli, and were told they could only march in the parade if they wore the uniforms of the Libyan army and march under the nation's green flag.

Several of the Nationalists agreed — some were even excited about getting to wear a uniform — but Wolfgang pointed out that the Libyan government supported the African National Congress that was fighting against white rule in South Africa and that the green flag was designed as a banner to indicate submission to Islam. After much heated discussion, he swayed the whole group to his side. They did not march.

When they flew back, Wolfgang noticed that there would be a stopover in Chicago. One of the conditions for his early release from prison was that he not re-enter the U.S. for five years, but it had only been a few months.

When the plane landed at O'Hare, Wolfgang refused to get off. The Alitalia pilot old him that if he didn't leave, he'd be charged with piracy. Wolfgang reluctantly went into the airport.

The Nationalists were rounded up, interrogated, strip- and cavity-searched and, except for Wolfgang, sent on their way. He was arrested for breach of court-ordered conditions.

Andrews sent money to defend him. Wolfgang said he got along with the first lawyer — a German-American — but "seized up" when he was replaced by a Jew. Despite the circumstances, the second lawyer helped him, securing his quick release for just $2,000.

American authorities drove Wolfgang to Niagara Falls, New York, where he boarded a bus to Toronto. He arrived at Andrews' Toronto house at 6 a.m., and was surprised to see an OPP officer with his old friend. The cop told Wolfgang that Andrews had nothing to do with his arrest, instead blaming it on one the Androids — unemployed men who lived in Andrews' massive home and ran his errands — who wanted to make a deal with the OPP in exchange for a new passport.

But the Libyan expedition had caused a major rift in the Nationalist Party.

Many blamed Andrews for their humiliating experiences at O'Hare, and were openly wondering why he would buddy up to a Muslim dictator who supported the ANC and other armed African groups anyway. When one of the members, James Dawson, was turned away from the U.S. border without explanation a few days later, several Nationalists decided that they must all be on a watch list.

The group began to splinter. Andrews retained some loyalists, but more people wanted to follow Wolfgang.

At a September 25, 1989 meeting with Gerald Lincoln, Grant Bristow and James Dawson, he founded the Heritage Front. Lincoln, who had the least legal baggage, would serve as president, but Wolfgang acknowledged that he and, to a lesser extent, Bristow would be pulling the strings. "I already had this idea for a number of years myself, but I said to them basically, 'Fine, but I'm not going to be the one who is going to do all the work. If I have the support of others, I am willing to form an organization, and if I don't, I'm not going to do it myself.'" Wolfgang said years later. "So, especially

Gerry Lincoln and Grant Bristow assured me that they would be totally supportive if I were to start an organization"

The organization consisted of a political wing that published a "pro-white" newsletter that was careful edited to prevent breaking any hate speech laws, and reached out to the KKK, Aryan Nations and other white supremacist groups in Canada.

But it also had a military wing, that Wolfgang described as being tasked to "clandestinely forward the white supremacist movement." That would be accomplished by robbing black drug dealers and, potentially, armored cars. Terrorist tactics would be used not against Jews and people of color, but rather whites who rejected white supremacist ideals — people he called "race traitors."

He also hoped that the Libyan government would pay him for information he had gained on Jewish organizations in Canada.

The master plan was to save enough money to establish their own town outside of Peterborough, and to provide it with pro-white bylaws.

Wolfgang didn't know it, but Canadian authorities had an undercover agent, Bristow, in his group, and were aware of his every move.

The Heritage Front's first action was more annoying than violent. TV Ontario aired a live panel discussion on racism and related issues, and the members of the Heritage Front managed to clog the phone lines and, when they got through, shout racist epithets.

The military wing didn't rob any drug dealers, but was kept busy providing security for white supremacists like Tom Metzger, Ernst Zündel and David Irving, along with more mainstream clients.

Among them were candidates and officials from the Reform Party. After two straight majority election wins, the Progressive Conservative party suffered a tremendous loss of popularity in the 1988 election, and was reduced to just two seats in parliament, and were no longer officially recognized as a party.

Many Canadian conservatives, especially in the West, threw their support behind the fledgling Reform Party, led by Preston Manning.

Members of the Heritage Front, including Wolfgang, provided security at Reform Party events in Ontario through Overfield's private bailiff company, always free of charge. Bristow even served as Manning's personal bodyguard at some events.

As they became more familiar to party officials, members of the Heritage Front provided other services, like signing up interested voters for mailing lists and distributing Reform Party campaign material.

And they also had their own projects. They started the Equal Rights for Whites Hotline (an innocuous-seeming 1-800 number that triggered a recorded speech espousing racist philosophies), invited more speakers, sent emissaries to Montreal and other Canadian cities and recruiters to local high schools.

That put them into conflict with the many anti-racist groups that were forming in response, and fistfights took place on many occasions.

They made headlines on May 18, 1992. The Morgentaler abortion clinic of Harbord Street was firebombed, and police had found Heritage Front-related graffiti at the scene. The bombing was never conclusively linked to the group, but the association gave their threats more credibility.

Things started to go downhill for the Heritage Front quickly in 1993, though. Under pressure from the media, the Reform Party expelled its members. A group called the Anti-Racist Alliance managed to hack the Equal Rights for Whites Hotline, and track down its location to the house of Heritage Front member Gary Schipper. After Schipper was assaulted and his house vandalized, Wolfgang and several other Heritage Front members went to Sneaky Dee's — a restaurant at the corner of College and Bathurst Streets where the members of several anti-racist organizations hung out — and got into a brawl with Anti-Racist Alliance supporters. Wolfgang went to jail for aggravated assault.

He went back to jail for contempt of court after he reactivated the Equal Rights for Whites Hotline despite losing suits brought by Jewish and Indigenous People's groups.

After his release, Wolfgang was deeply disillusioned. Details revealed in his aggravated assault trial let him know there was an undercover agent in the Heritage Front, and his convictions led the province to repeal his bailiff's license. He disbanded the Heritage Front, and started to traffic cigarettes, drugs and stolen cars as a career. In 1998, he went to jail again when he was stopped by police while driving a stolen car.

With little else to do, Wolfgang retired from the public eye and sold drugs out of his tiny apartment in Scarborough. Neighbors at 2 North Drive — and it must've bothered Wolfgang that so many of them were people of color — knew there was something going on with the weird old guy in Apartment 207 who never seemed to leave, but constantly received visitors at any hour of the day or night.

On the morning of April 13, 2005, Wolfgang got a call from one of his regular customers, 43-year-old Keith Deroux. Keith asked him, in code, if he had any cocaine. Wolfgang replied that he might, if Keith was able to come up with the $305 he owed him. Keith assured Wolfgang that he had the cash and would be over as soon as he could.

At about 2:30 in the afternoon, Wolfgang — dressed only in a T-shirt and boxer shorts, as had become his norm — answered a knock at the door. It was Keith, and he was in bad shape. Suffering from methadone withdrawal, he fortified himself that day with Jack Daniel's, Tylenol tablets with codeine and a snort of coke.

It was odd that Keith would show up in person. He didn't like Wolfgang, and usually sent someone else over to pick up product. He was shivering in the hallway and had a trail of dried blood on his upper lip when Wolfgang invited him in.

Wolfgang kept his weed in his fridge and his cocaine in a closet, and he knew which one Keith was after. As Wolfgang headed to the closet, his back turned to his client, Keith pulled a .22-caliber Röhm Gesellschaft revolver out of his trendy Pan-Am shoulder bag.

When Wolfgang turned around and saw the gun, he dropped the coke and put his hands in the air. Keith asked him if he was alone in the apartment. Wolfgang said that he was. Keith, clearly paranoid, told Wolfgang to stay in the bedroom while he searched the closet.

He said he was looking for someone hiding in it, but even the most cursory glance would have revealed anyone hiding in the small, cluttered space.

It was while Keith had his head in the closet — yelling at Wolfgang, accusing him of bugging his apartment and putting other people's coke purchases on his tab — that Wolfgang ran from the bedroom and out the apartment door.

Keith shot at him, missing twice, as Wolfgang made his way to the building's primary stairwell. Unwisely, Wolfgang stopped and turned to see if Keith was chasing him. That gave Keith a clear shot and he finally hit his target, but it was just a glancing blow, searing through some flesh on the side of Wolfgang's chest. The older man started to run again, but fell face-first to the wall-to-wall carpeting as Keith's fourth shot hit him in the back of the head.

Instead of fleeing, Keith went back into No. 207. When he heard sirens, he locked himself inside. Police arrived very quickly, and ordered him to come out. But he warned them that he was armed and unwilling to surrender.

A three-hour standoff ensued, which ended only when the police managed to get his brother, via telephone, to convince him to give himself up.

Reporters on the scene recognized the name of the deceased, and asked police if Wolfgang's notorious past had anything to do with the incident. "There's no information that would indicate that the homicide had anything to do with Mr. Droege's political activity," Detective Sergeant Peter Callaghan replied after his investigation. "The information provided to us leads us to believe that it had nothing to do with that."

Instead, a different story unraveled. Deroux had a long history of violent events and drug abuse. After it was revealed that his half-brother Colin McGregor had been convicted of murdering his wife with a crossbow in 1991, his cousin Whitney Deroux told reporters: "It just seems that I don't know what it is with the Deroux, but trouble follows, I guess it runs in the genes."

Callaghan also revealed that Keith was living with Nicola Slyford, a woman who had previously been in a relationship with Wolfgang, and that he was very jealous.

Keith was originally charged with second-degree murder, but agreed to plead guilty to a manslaughter charge. At his sentencing, his lawyers revealed that he was suffering from paranoid delusions that he was under very sophisticated surveillance by a complex network in his home, on his computer and on his phone. He believed that gasses were pumped into his bedroom every night and that there was an underground tunnel that spies used to enter his apartment. While pondering his situation, he became convinced that the only person he knew with enough funds and wherewithal to carry off such an operation was Wolfgang, so he decided he had to kill him.

Keith was sentenced to ten years minus credit for time served.

Of course, that is — as his supporters would claim — just the official story. White supremacist forums and chat rooms and other modes of social media were, and still are, alive with other theories. Those who accept that Keith killed Wolfgang often say that he is a Jew, a "half-breed," a Mafiosi or even a spy. Many deny Wolfgang sold drugs and some say that Keith received a light sentence in exchange for doing the government a favor.

In the opinion of the courts and mainstream media, Wolfgang was a racist criminal who was killed by an addict who was addled by the very drugs Wolfgang supplied him with. But in the eyes of his supporters, he was kindly old Uncle Wolf, a clean-living man who stuck to what he believed in and was assassinated for his views.

Note: I frequently use the phrase white supremacist to describe Droege and his allies. They deny that title. Droege himself wrote in a sworn affidavit that: "I am not a white supremacist. We are racial nationalists whose eventual goal would be the creation of an exclusively white state for those wishing to live in an area among their own kind." But that seems like splitting hairs. So, for the purpose of this book, anyone who advocates for the separation of races for the benefit of white people fulfils the definition of white supremacist, even though they prefer "white nationalist" or "white preservationist."

Chapter 9

Summertime Bash

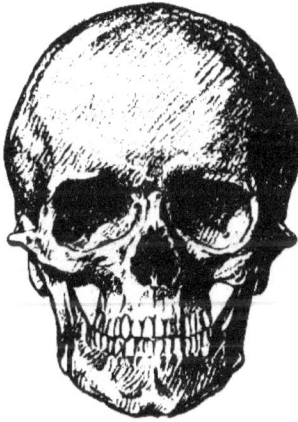

B eing gay in Toronto wasn't always the way it is now. For decades, people — particularly men — who were thought to be part of the LGBQT community were subject to insults, cat-calls and even physical abuse on a regular basis.

There was even a long-standing tradition of mobs gathering outside suspected gay bars every Halloween to throw eggs and invective at their patrons on their way in and out. It wasn't broken up until 1981, when the activist Right to Privacy Committee established the Gay Street Patrol — a group of dedicated men and women who did their best to oppose such gatherings, prevent assaults against LGBQT people and help any victims they found — started interfering.

The police weren't much help. They were arresting gay men for soliciting sex in public places, private clubs and even through classified ads. The Body Politic, Toronto's first LGBQT-oriented newspaper, was raided frequently by police, losing not just files and data, but the equipment they needed to publish.

And it was in that environment Kenneth Zeller lived. Actually, Zeller had it a little tougher than most. He was not just openly gay, he was a public school teacher and librarian, and many people at the time thought that those occupations were not suitable for LGBQT people. They didn't want their kids recruited by or even exposed to people with such lifestyles.

But Zeller soldiered on, and was — from all accounts — competent and well-liked in both roles. In fact, he had been president of the Toronto Teacher-Librarian Association.

And he was active in his community. Not just the LGBQT community, but the larger one. He was such an ardent supporter of and campaigner for the National Ballet Company that they gave him an award for his efforts. He taught figure skating and volunteered with Inner City Angels, an activist group that helps disadvantaged youth. And he still found time to pursue a master's degree.

It was the end of the 1984-85 school year, and time to celebrate. And it was expected to be a busy weekend for Kenn. On Friday, June 21, he and his school colleagues were going to have a party, and on Saturday, he was going to have an even bigger blast. His 40th birthday had been on June 5, but he and his friends had delayed the festivities until after the school year, so on the 22nd, they — and Kenn was proud to have close friends from both inside and outside the LGBQT community — were going to usher him into middle age.

After the party with school staff on Friday night, Kenn — who had downed a few drinks — went off on his own. Although he was in a steady relationship, Kenn would sometimes go looking for sex with other men. At the time, many gay men would take part in what was called "cruising" — walking around places known to be frequented by other gay men, finding a partner, agreeing to sex and then hooking up, usually in a public restroom. Of course, cruising still exists, but at a time when the police were doing their best to shut down every other way for gay men to meet, it was rampant.

Kenn knew of a few spots, and decided on High Park in the city's West End. Because he was from the other side of town, the chances of running into someone he knew were slim, and it was a nice environment with old trees and ponds.

He parked his Audi on the East side of Colborne Lodge Drive, one of the curving roads through the park. He took a popper — bottled amyl nitrate, a substance many, especially those in the LGBQT community, believe enhances sex when inhaled — out of his glove compartment and put it in his shirt pocket. He then took his wallet out of his pants pocket and put it in his trunk. High Park wasn't considered that dangerous a place, but it wasa Saturday night and he was alone. Having someone mug him or break into his car would put a real damper on what was supposed to be a big weekend.

But gay men weren't the only ones who knew about cruising back in 1985, or where it happened.

While Kenn was partying with his pals from Williamson Road Junior Public School that night, eight high school students who often played hockey together — Richard Bauer, 16; Michael Burak, 16; Henry Juszczuk, 16; Steven Christou, 16; Michael Bedard, 17; and three others who can't be named — were having some celebrations of their own.

The Beer Store, still called the Brewers' Retail back in 1985, wasn't picky about I.D. back then and the boys had no problem buying a case of beer. They went to Port Credit's Jack Darling Memorial Park to drink it because they had heard that some of their friends would be there, and it looked like it might become quite the party.

It had indeed grown to be a huge bash, and the Peel Police felt the need to sweep and close the park at 9:15 that evening because neighbors were complaining about loud parties with teenagers drinking and fighting and doing God knows what.

Disappointed, the group of eight got back in their van, and headed east, back into Toronto. They stopped behind a gas station to drink more beer and eat some burgers and fries they had picked up from Harvey's along the way.

While they were there, the conversation turned to the inevitable question of what they were going to do for the rest of the night. Not only were they bored, but they were out of beer. They could probably buy more, except they were also out of cash.

That's when one of them, it was never determined who, came up with a plan that would solve both problems. "Let's get money from a queer!" he shouted. The first response, again from a person whose identity was never revealed, was: "Let's beat up a fag!" The rest of the group offered little other than "yeah" or "fuck yeah."

While that might sound like an odd idea to build a quick consensus for, the tenor of the times was different. Many boys were taught to fear gay men because much of the community linked homosexuality with pedophilia. As boys grew bigger and more aggressive, that fear often morphed into contempt. Gay men, especially those cruising, were considered ideal targets. By the definition of cruising, they were alone and vulnerable. And the belief among many was that gay men were easy to intimidate — whether physically or by threat of exposure — and tended to have lots of money.

For some, the chance to rob and assault someone from a group they hated and was unlikely to put up much of a fight added nothing more than excitement to the night.

Or, as many close to the case maintain, the boys did intend to rob someone that night and were prepared to use violence, but the words "fag" and "queer" were simply insulting terms, and the boys did not mean to specifically target homosexuals.

At any rate, the boys got back into their van and headed to High Park, which was in their home neighborhood. They all knew which part of the big park the cruising went on in. It was primarily centered around the since-closed public restrooms in the southeast corner of the park.

The boys parked the van not far from Kenn's Audi, and then went wandering around, looking for a man.

Kenn was also looking for a man, and thought he found one in Burak. The teacher approached the young man, intent on striking up a conversation. But as soon as he was within a few feet, Burak shouted "You fucking faggot!" and threw the much slighter man to the ground.

Upon hearing the attack, Bauer, Juszczuk, Christou and Bedard came running.

Kenn managed to get up and took off towards his car. In the chaos, he lost a shoe, slowing him down.

He made it to the Audi and was struggling to unlock it when Bedard — the biggest and most athletic of the bunch — punched him in the face, knocking him to the ground. Bedard told Kenn to give him all his money. Kenn said that he didn't have any. Bedard opened the car door and shoved Kenn into the front seat.

At the same time, Christou smashed the passenger-side window, unlocked the door, jumped into the car and started punching Kenn in the head.

Bauer took out a knife and slashed three of the Audi's tires and smashed the back windows.

One particularly hard blow from Christou sent Kenn reeling, and his head was hanging out the driver-side door. Burak then delivered a devastating kick to the back of Kenn's cranium.

The five boys continued to pummel the unconscious man until, for reasons never publicly revealed, they stopped. They left the bloodied and broken school teacher and returned to their three other friends who had been watching from a distance. They all then separated and made their individual ways home.

When Christou arrived home some time after 3 a.m., his mom made him two bacon and cheese sandwiches, which he polished off with a can of store-brand cola.

Before that, however, just a few minutes after the attack, a 28-year-old man who was also walking through that part of the park saw a car with its front doors open. As he got closer, he saw that it had a smashed rear window. As he drew even closer, he saw that a man was hanging out of it. He could tell that Kenn was in pretty bad shape, unconscious and bleeding badly. Without delay, he ran to a nearby payphone and called 911. He then returned to the Audi and waited for an ambulance to arrive.

Kenn was rushed to St. Joseph's Hospital about four blocks away. But it was too late. He was declared dead at 1:09 on Saturday morning.

The investigation did not take long. Unbeknownst to the boys, the attack had been watched, and two men who were in the area that night went to police and told them what they had seen and heard. That gave the cops a general idea of who the culprits were, and when they produced fingerprints, they rounded up all eight boys from the group, and questioned them.

Three of them told the same story; that they were along for the ride, they saw what happened, but they did not participate. They were free to go, but were expected to testify against the other five.

Burak, Bauer, Juszczuk, Christou and Bedard also told basically the same story. They had been part of the group that had assaulted and killed Kenn, but each of them took great pains to incriminate the others, while proclaiming their own innocence.

All five were charged with first-degree murder and held without bail. The judge at their bail hearing ordered a publication ban because all the accused were under 18.

After word of the arrests made its way around school, Stephen Baker, also 16, told the police that his lifelong best friend Juszczuk had called him the Monday after the incident and asked him to meet with him in his backyard. Baker, intrigued, had no reason to decline. When he arrived, Juszczuk just stared at it him and wouldn't talk. Baker coaxed him to reveal his big secret, saying "C'mon, it can't be that bad."

But it was. Juszczuk told him: "We killed somebody."

Baker didn't believe it. "You're joking," he said, and went home. But he couldn't stop thinking about it, and when he heard that Juszczuk and his other pals had been arrested, he went to his parents and then the police with his story.

The Crown decided to reduce the charge to second-degree murder, but filed a motion to have the five tried as adults because the heinous nature of their alleged crime warranted something more severe than the three years in a youth institution that would be the maximum sentence allowed if they were tried as juveniles. It was granted.

Three days later, on November 25, 1985, all five of the group signed an agreed-upon statement of facts and pleaded guilty to manslaughter. The Crown accepted the deal because, he said, he did not believe the boys had intended to kill Kenn, just to rob him.

Their sentencing hearing started the next day. Their attorneys collected more than two dozen character witnesses — including Baker, who wept throughout his testimony. They uniformly praised the boys as kind and loving. All of them claimed under oath that the boys had no hatred for members of the LGBQT community. Their hockey coach admitted that he had often heard the boys call one another "gay" or "fag," but explained that they only used those words or similar references to indicate a clumsy play, and "never out of hostility."

Two psychologists who examined the boys said that alcohol was the factor that pushed them over the edge, not hatred of gay men.

When asked why the boys targeted a "fag" or "queer," they both responded that those were societal cues, that those words were often used as insults and did not always indicate that the person in question was indeed a homosexual.

When pressed with the fact that the boys intentionally went to a place where they knew gay men frequented when they were looking for a victim, Dr. Clive Chamberlain said that the boys were angered by "public displays of affection" in "what they considered to be their park" and said that he felt they also would have "taunted" a traditional male-female couple in the same situation.

The Crown asked for sentences ranging from 11 to 15 years, depending on the individual's involvement in the beating. Justice Gregory T. Evans, however, sided with the defense, sentencing each of the boys to nine years, regardless of their role in the killing. In his summation, he told them: "It worries me that young people like you pass judgement on someone like Kenneth Zeller and perform an execution because you believed he was a homosexual."

After the case was over, Kenn's death was tossed about as a political football, especially among school trustees in the city. Alex Chumak, who boasted in his campaign literature about having killed a proposed gay liaison committee for the very school the boys attended, led those who claimed it was alcohol that led the boys to kill, while others said it was their cultural hatred of LGBQT people.

Eventually, the Toronto District School Board approved gay liaisons in school, and other programs to help promote a better understanding of and more tolerance for LGBQT lifestyles.

Chapter 10

Manhunt in the Arctic

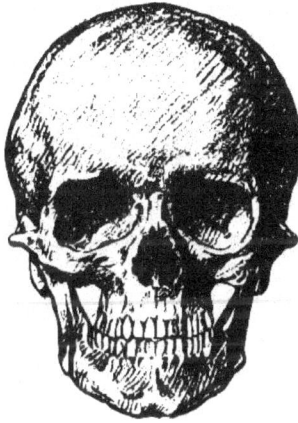

W hen word got back to Fort Norman in 1915 that an Inuit man had been seen wearing priests' cassocks up in Coppermine, the men there feared the worst.

In the summer of 1913, two priests had left Fort Norman (now called Tulita, Northwest Territories) to make the arduous journey around Great Bear Lake and beyond the tree line to Coppermine (now Kugluktuk, Nunavut) on the shore of the Arctic Ocean. They had not been heard from since.

Correctly assuming that the priests would not have given up their cassocks willingly, the traders in Fort Norman contacted the Catholic Diocese who then pushed the North-West Mounted Police to investigate.

The priests were soldiers in a war of sorts. Both Catholic and Protestant missionaries had been competing for the souls among Canada's native people, and both were working furiously to add as many converts as possible. So when rumors of an Anglican minister appearing not far from Coppermine emerged, the Catholic church decided it must send its own representatives to the area as quickly as they could.

And there was a particular interest in the Coppermine area. The people who live there — the Copper Inuit — were sometimes referred to as the "Blonde Eskimos" because of occasional sightings of light-haired and even light-eyed individuals. Many people back then believed them to be of European or partially European stock, which, at the time, made them even more desirable to the churches.

The missing missionaries were oblates, those who follow the rules of a monastic order without actually being monks themselves. The more veteran of the two was Father Jean-Baptiste Rouvière. He had served four years ministering to the Tlicho (also known as

Dogrib) and Sahtu (also known as Hareskin or North Slavey) —
Athabaskan-speaking Dene people with a very different lifestyle and
a long-standing ethnic feud with the Inuit. Rouvière was a tough little
man, who barely cleared five feet tall, and had a long beard.

He had been joined by Father Guillaume LeRoux, who was
described as a well-educated gentleman who was bedeviled by a hot
and unpredictable temper. He was a big man, over six feet tall and
wore a short beard.

After prodding by the Catholic church, the NWMP struggled to
find a suitable investigator. One of their officers in Regina, Charles
Deering "Denny" LaNauze, had considerable experience in the
Northwest Territories (but no previous contact with the Inuit). He
seemed like the best choice, but was preparing to leave the force to
fight in the First World War.

The NWMP convinced him to take on the case instead and
promoted him to Inspector. He and two constables (J.E.F. White
and D. Withers) met in Edmonton and made their way to Fort
Norman. From there, he recruited a priest, Father Frapsance (often
spelled in records as Frapsauce), several men he described as
"Indians" and another man, D'Arcy Arden, who was familiar with
the area, but did not speak Inuktitut well enough to translate. And,
even though he was hundreds of miles away from the nearest Inuit
settlement, LaNauze was lucky enough to meet and recruit an Inuit
interpreter named Ilavinik. He and Arden were made temporary
special constables for the investigation. Ilavinik also brought along
his wife, Mamayak, and daughter, Nagosak.

The team left Fort Norman on July 23, 1915. After an arduous
journey by canoe and York boat (small steamboats used mainly by
the Hudson's Bay Company), on September 28, the party had
discovered the priests' cabin on the shores of what is now called
Lake Rouvier in honor of Rouvière, just north of the tree line.
LaNauze described the tiny dwelling as being "in ruins," and wrote
that it:

"… appears to have been ruthlessly destroyed, half the
roof was burned away and the debris from it covered the

floor. There was nothing movable left. The door was missing."

The men searched the area intensely, but could find no indication of the priests' whereabouts. They recovered some items that were at least a year old, including an Inuit shoe, a copper-tipped arrow of the type frequently used by the people in the area where the Inuit men wearing cassocks were reported and a spent .44-caliber cartridge. LaNauze knew that the priests had taken a Mauser .44 rifle along with them, but it was not found at the site. They also discovered some newer items, including deer bones and firewood, that indicated someone had used the shelter more recently.

With winter approaching and the supply of caribou dwindling due to their migration, LaNauze and his party — minus Frapsance, who returned to Fort Norman — camped out until spring. Over that period, LaNauze and Ilavinik became good friends and LaNauze wrote back to his superiors back at Fort Norman that "Eskimo cannot be treated on the footing of master and servant."

The investigators finally arrived at Coppermine on April 30, 1916. At first, LaNauze found the people of Coppermine reluctant to speak about the case. A few years earlier, an English explorer and undeniable eccentric named John Hornby had warned that if an Inuit had killed a white man, that the whole community would be exterminated.

It wasn't true. In 1912, two Inuit men killed two explorers — Harry V. Radford and Thomas George Street — at nearby Bathurst Inlet. The NWMP investigated, found their suspects and gained confessions, but, after pressure from Ottawa, let them go. Instead, they issued a public warning that, from that point forward, Inuit would have to obey Canadian law or be punished accordingly. But most of the people of Coppermine didn't know about that case, and many of them still believed Hornby's threat.

The investigators combed the area by dogsled, but came up with nothing that they could connect to the priests. On May 1, they came upon a village called Kugaryuak. Arden had visited before, and the people there were happy to see him again and inquired about potential trade. LaNauze told them through Ilavinik that they weren't there to trade, but that the "Big White Chief" had sent him to "look after them" and to teach them right from wrong. He made a point of not mentioning the missing priests right away because he wanted to gain their trust.

Upon hearing that there were other white men in the area, LaNauze went to look for them, leaving Ilavinik behind to ask questions.

On May 3, LaNauze met another NWMP officer, Corporal Wyndham Valentine Bruce at a research camp not far from the village. Bruce had been accompanying anthropologists Vilhjalmur Stefansson and Diamond Jenness and biologist Rudolph Martin Anderson when he heard about the case and volunteered to help. Bruce was deeply saddened to hear about the ransacked cabin, as he had held out hope that the priests were still alive.

Although it has been reported in media that the two officers were bitter rivals, personal correspondence between the two and others strongly indicates that they actually worked together well and on a friendly basis. LaNauze valued Bruce's familiarity with the area and people and praised his tact, writing: "none of the natives were suspicious of his presence in the gulf, and he had much valuable information for me, knew the country, and knew practically all the Eskimos."

Bruce had already been conducting his own investigation. Careful not to indicate what he was doing to the local people, he casually asked questions and bought everything he could find that he thought could be linked to the missing priests. He stopped at the .44 rifle, though, because there were several in the village and he could not determine which, if any, had belonged to the priests.

LaNauze asked him about the cassocks. Bruce told him that an Inuit man named Uluksuk had been seen wearing one, and that Bruce had managed to steal it as evidence. From Bruce's description, LaNauze decided that it was the same man his Athabaskan-speaking witnesses had called Dloogaa. Uluksuk lived in Inuaireneruit, a larger village not far away.

LaNauze and Bruce returned to Kugaryuak to find that Ilavinik had found out a great deal about the locals' habits and had even been told by an elder named Koglouga that the priests' cabin had been intentionally burned.

In lnuaireneruit, the party was given another warm welcome, but LaNauze found the people less inclined to talk. He was particularly suspicious of one man named Kormik, who talked about his travels to Great Bear Lake, but said he had seen no white men there.

LaNauze also began to suspect that two brothers, Nachin and Ekkeshuina, were hiding something when he found out they frequently hunted very close to the destroyed cabin.

Ilavinik was also suspicious and thought he could get more information out of the men. He arranged to talk with them in their snow house. LaNauze "sat back and watched" as Ilavinik questioned the men for five minutes or so, and knew something was up when he saw Ilavinik's hands begin to tremble. Finally, he turned to LaNauze and told him "I got him, the priests were killed by Uluksuk, all right; these men very, very sorry." The inspector reported that Nachin and Ekkeshuina covered their faces in shame.

LaNauze rushed out of the house to inform Bruce. When he returned, there was a crowd inside. Ilavinik told him "now you write down these two names Uluksuk and Sinnisiak, you got that? Now I find out some more."

Then the interpreter-turned-special constable ordered the collected people to be quiet and let Koeha, an elder who appeared to Ilavinik to have the most information, speak. He spoke until 4 a.m.

In November 1913, he said, the priests left lnuaireneruit after a few uneventful days there. Two days later, Uluksuk and Sinnisiak said they would follow them to see if they needed any help. A few days after that, Uluksuk and Sinnisiak returned to lnuaireneruit with the priests' clothes and rifle. When people asked them how they got the items, they told them, without hesitation, that they had killed the priests.

Koeha recounted that Uluksuk had explained how it all went down. He told him that the killings were Sinnisiak's idea and that he was urged to cooperate. He said that Sinnisiak had stabbed Le Roux in the back and that Uluksuk finished him off with an axe blow to the head. Upon seeing the melee, Rouvière made a dash for his rifle, which was bound to a nearby sled. But Sinnisiak beat him to it and shot the fleeing oblate in the back. He fell, but was struggling to get back up when Sinnisiak and Uluksuk caught up to him and stabbed him repeatedly until he was dead.

After the two priests were dead, Koeha said that Uluksuk cut into LeRoux's belly and ate part of his liver then gave another portion to Sinnisiak, who ate it. It was a tradition among the people of the area to eat a portion of any animal they killed at the scene of the hunt. Over the years, the Inuit have been accused — mainly by Europeans — of cannibalism, but actual records are extremely rare. As historian Rachel Qitsualik-Tinsley wrote: "the stories of true cannibalism … are obviously cases of isolated, monstrous behavior, rather than of monstrous culture."

Upon hearing the story, Koeha recruited three men to investigate. They found the crime scene at a place appropriately named Bloody Falls. He described it:

> "When we got to the place I saw one man dead lying by the sled, it was Ilogoak (LeRoux), and I cried. I did not see Kuleavik (Rouvière); the snow had covered Ilogoak's face all but his nose; he was lying on his back beside the sled, with his head up. The man that had killed him and cut up his breast and all inside was cut up with a knife."

When they returned, Koeha asked Uluksuk why he killed the priests.

"I did not want to kill them," Uluksuk answered. "Sinnisiak told me to kill them."

Koeha asked Uluksuk if he ate any part of the priests. The killer sheepishly answered "I eat some of his guts."

Koeha went on to say that the whole village had been saddened by the news, as they considered LeRoux and Rouvière to be "good white men" and valued their trade and what they taught.

Another man from the village, Hupo, reported to LaNauze that the priests did their job:

"These two men were telling us about the land above the skies. They showed us colored pictures of Heaven, and they said that after we died we would go there. They used to sing just like the Eskimos when they make medicine. They held our hands and taught us to make the sign of the Cross, and they put a little bread sometimes in my mouth."

LaNauze urged Ilavinik to ask Koeha why nobody had reported the murders to Canadian authorities. Koeha said that, at first, they were afraid because of Hornby's warning, but that the collective guilt was so bad they had tried to tell Arden and his men on an earlier visit, but they could not get the message across because of language differences.

The next day, LaNauze set out to find Sinnisiak. Not only was he alleged to be the primary assailant, he also had a reputation for violence. Hupo told LaNauze "Sinnisiak is a bad man, everyone says so, and he told me lies."

Another man, Uluksuk Mayuk, not to be confused with the suspect Uluksak, told LaNauze:

"I found the place where the two white men were killed after looking a long time with my father and wives. First, I found the sled and then I found a man's jaw bone close to it. My father was very sorry and put it away on a high place. The other body was a little way off in a creek. I saw some clothing; the mud had covered it up. The bones may be there now; I know the place and I will take you to it."

Several local people had told the inspector that Sinnisiak was hunting on the ice near Victoria Island.

They went out to find him after Bruce formally wrote up the charges. Fog caused LaNauze to call back his first attempt, but on his second, his guides took him through a series of deserted encampments on their way to Sinnisiak's suspected location. One of the snow houses had been lived in recently, and it caused LaNauze to wonder if Sinnisiak had heard about the investigation and was on the run.

On May 15, they came upon a village of about 40 people living in skin houses. After the initial excitement of greeting strangers, the locals were questioned. A guide, Uluksuk Mayuk, surreptitiously swept the village and told LaNauze that he had not seen Sinnisiak, but had seen his wife. Mayuk, LaNauze, Ilavinik and White entered the tent where the guide had seen Sinnisiak's wife. Inside there was a man making a bow. When he saw the men enter, he "appeared to be stunned with fear" and later told LaNauze that he expected them to kill him on the spot.

They arrested him and searched the tent, finding a loaded .22-caliber rifle and two knives hidden under a caribou pelt.

Sinnisiak appeared to be confused. He asked Ilavinik what was going on. The special constable told him "the white men here want you to go with them."

He told LaNauze that Sinnisiak replied: "If the white men kill me. I will make medicine and their ship will go down in the ice and all will be drowned."

As people poured into the tent, Sinnisiak got more and more nervous, visibly trembling. It was not until other members of the crowd urged him to go that he stood up and agreed to surrender. LaNauze, always trying to avert intensifying situations, said he could bring his wife along if he wanted.

A subsequent search of the camp uncovered the priests' Mauser. It and been bought and sold many times over, and LaNauze was forced to trade a new and far superior .30-30 Winchester to Kormik, its most recent owner, for the evidence.

On the following day, the team and suspect arrived in Bernard Harbour (also known as Nulahugiuq, Nunavut). The police all took turns guarding Sinnisiak. The prisoner refused to sleep because, he told Ilavinik, he was sure he would be stabbed in his sleep.

Despite being carefully warned twice that his words could be used against him, Sinnisiak said he wanted to tell his story. He claimed that the priests had beaten him and Uluksak, and threatened to shoot them; so he decided to kill them before they killed him. He said that Kormik had earlier floated the idea of killing them because he thought LeRoux was a cruel man and that he wanted his rifle.

LaNauze charged Sinnisiak with two counts of second-degree murder.

Now he had to find Uluksak. He had information that the suspect was planning to head to the Dismal Lake district to hunt caribou and that his best bet was to find him at the mouth of the Coppermine River where hunters gathered to socialize, trade and claim hunting territories.

LaNauze, Ilavinik, Wight and a half-Inuit guide named Patsy Klenkenberg (who knew Uluksak) arrived at the spot on May 17. They had made it there before any hunters had gathered, but Klenkenberg, using his ilgaak (Inuit snow goggles), managed to spot six distant dogsleds approaching slowly. They disappeared behind an island about ten miles away, and it was not until May 22 that a sled arrived at the mouth of the Coppermine. On it were a man named Angebrunna and his wife. Angebrunna also knew Uluksak and said that he was on one of the six sleds that had stopped at the island.

The investigators took off for the island as quickly as they could. When they arrived, they were greeted by several Inuit people who had their hands over their heads in what LaNauze took to be an international "peace sign." It was only when he and his crew did the same that they approached.

All but one. A man Klenkenberg recognized as Uluksak stayed behind, his head lowered.

Finally, Uluksak raised his hands and ran toward the party, shouting something that Ilavinik translated as "thank you, I'm glad."

Uluksak admitted that he knew why they were there and asked if LaNauze and Wight were going to kill him or just hit him on the head like the other white men had. LaNauze did his best to reassure the suspect that they were not there to hurt him, but that he had to go with them. Uluksak said that he would go wherever they wanted him to, but asked if they could wait until after his wife had finished making him a new pair of waterproof boots.

LaNauze wrote back to Fort Norman that Uluksak was a very different type of man than Sinnisiak, and did not seem at all violent. He was armed, but with just a hunting bow and a few arrows.

Uluksuk's pregnant wife became very upset when she found out what was going on, but LaNauze calmed her by giving her a folding tent, a cup and some matches. He also implored the rest of the hunters to help her with food.

LaNauze, Klenkenberg and the prisoner headed to Bernard Harbour to meet up with Bruce and Sinnisiak, while White and some guides headed back to the crime scene to gather more data. LaNauze wrote: "The prisoner gave no trouble en route and was cheerful and willing."

When they arrived, LaNauze, through Ilavinik, warned Uluksak twice that his words could be used against him and that it might be unwise to talk. But the suspect insisted he wanted to tell the story. His account was very similar to Sinnisiak's, except that he claimed that every violent act he took part in was at Sinnisiak's urging.

LaNauze noted that Uluksak was trembling and agitated under questioning, but returned to his "customary spirits" after he was finished.

LaNauze then charged him with two counts of second-degree murder.

He then accepted a ride on the American Coast Guard ship Alaska, which would pick them up at Herschel Island, in the Arctic Ocean just north of the Yukon. Not only would the trip be faster and less arduous, but LaNauze feared losing one or both of the prisoners on a long overland journey and several of the Inuit involved, including the prisoners, expressed concerns about their safety while passing through Dene territory.

LaNauze reported that: "The prisoners are now in good health and are cheerful and willing, and are quick to pick up our ways. Sinnisiak is inclined to be nervous, but Uluksuk does not seem to worry in the least" and he had no concerns about either trying to escape.

The Crown decided to try only Sinnisiak, and just for the murder of Rouvière. Sinnisiak's trial began in Edmonton on August 14,

1917. Prosecutor Charles Cursolles McCaul made no bones about why he felt the case was serious:

> "You, gentlemen, can understand how important this is: white men travel through the barren lands; white men live on the shores of Bear Lake; white men go to the shores of the Arctic Ocean; and if we are to believe the reports of the copper deposits near the mouth of the Coppermine River, many white men more may go to investigate and to work the mines. The Eskimo must be made to understand that the lives of others are sacred, and that they are not justified in killing on account of any mere trifle that may ruffle or annoy them."

The accused and Uluksuk, who was there as a witness, wore their caribou skin clothes (including their parkas) throughout the trial and were given a tub of ice water in case they became too hot indoors. Both fell asleep frequently during the trial.

His attorney, James Wallbridge, argued at length not only just that Sinnisiak feared for his own life because the priests had been threatening and he killed in self-defense, but he also pointed out that the suspect was totally unaware of Canadian law and should not be judged by it.

After the judge actually urged the jury to find Sinnisiak guilty, they deliberated for an hour and came back with a verdict of not guilty.

Shocked, Sinnisiak shouted "It is not true. I did kill him!"

McCaul and Justice Horace Harvey were outraged. McCaul later blamed the local media for the acquittal, saying that they had stirred up enough anti-Catholic sentiment that it was impossible for the killer of a priest to get a fair trial in Edmonton.

But that didn't mean that the two Inuit men were free. McCaul then filed to Harvey for a trial for both of them for the murder of LeRoux and asked for a change of venue. Harvey granted both requests.

That trial started August 22 in Calgary. McCaul argued that it was important for Canadian law to be enforced throughout Canada. He, did, however, ask for clemency in their sentence so that they could return to their community to teach others about "British justice" and "civilization." After 45 minutes of deliberation, the jury found both men to be guilty.

They were sentenced by Harvey (who later became Chief Justice of Alberta) in Edmonton on October 15. Pointing out that the only legal sentence in Canada for murder was death, he sentenced them to be hanged.

The men were taken first to a prison in Yukon and then to Fort Resolution on the southern shore of Great Slave Lake, where a local court commuted their sentences to imprisonment. They never spent any time behind bars there, though; instead they served their sentences as handymen and janitors at the local trading post. They were officially described as "model prisoners" by the local NWMP detachment.

After they agreed to help establish a new NWMP detachment at Tree River, Northwest Territories, serving as dogsled drivers, they were allowed to return to their home community on May 15, 1919.

It has been frequently reported, even in the Canadian Encyclopedia, that the two became wealthy and began to bully other people in their community, but it's not true. The myth began in 1924 when a true story involving a woman named Ikayena, who killed a man named Uluksuk in a dispute over a dog, became the subject of rumor, gossip and, eventually, news. But it was a different man in a different community.

In 1928, when the first Anglican Bishop of the Arctic, Archibald Lang Fleming, was touring the Coppermine area, he came across the Uluksuk who had been involved in the priests' murders. The man he found was riddled with tuberculosis and unable to hunt or otherwise take care of himself. Concerned, Fleming arranged to have him taken to a hospital in Aklavik, Northwest Territories.

The staff there was, however, unable to help him, so he returned to his home community aboard a Hudson's Bay ship, the S.S. Baychimo, and died in September 1929 at just 42 years old.

Sinnisiak died the following year. History does not record a definitive cause, but some sources indicate tuberculosis killed him too.

Note: Many prefer the spelling of Uluksuk to be Uloqsaq.

Chapter 11

They Called Them the Boyd Gang

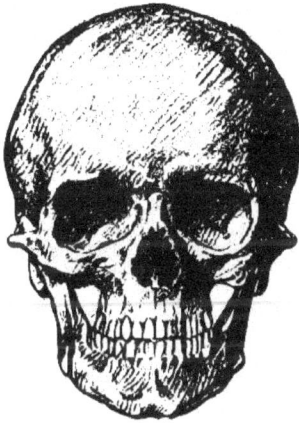

Nobody, but nobody, was cooler than the French Foreign Legion back in 1928. Not cowboys or fighter pilots or gangsters or the guys who put them in jail.

The French Foreign Legion was a romantic subject of novels, movies and the imaginations of boys everywhere. They were men who fought their way around the world; strong, independent and fierce. Better yet, they were real, and word was that the Legion would give any able-bodied man a shot, no matter who he was, where he was from or what his circumstances were.

That suited Eddie Boyd just fine. He was a mischievous kid, prone to sneaking out of church and stealing things from families he knew weren't home. He wanted to become a professional singer, but never got a gig better than the Danforth YMCA.

He thought Toronto was boring. Nothing ever happened there. It was so straight-laced that they even locked up the swings in the park on Sundays. That's how far they'd go to keep anyone from having any fun.

And that suited Eddie's father just fine. Edwin Glover Boyd was a strict disciplinarian who found his inspiration in the Bible — almost always the fire and brimstone of the Old Testament and never the redemption and forgiveness of the New Testament.

After returning from the First World War when Eddie was just a toddler, he became a street cop. Glover dispensed hard-hearted justice — not just of the city's laws but also what he interpreted as God's — on the street and at home.

And that was more than 14-year-old Edwin Alonzo "Eddie" Boyd thought he could stand. He had to come up with a plan. He couldn't just run away; his dad was a veteran cop who knew everybody. Eddie would be dragged home, humiliated and punished, and life would get even worse. If he wanted to join the French Foreign Legion, he decided, he'd have to fake his own death.

So, on a summer day when he knew a storm was approaching, he took his bike down to the beach. He left his sneakers and a pile of his clothes beside his bike, careful to place a slip of paper with his name and address in the breast pocket of the shirt. Then he started walking east.

The Toronto police had been dragging the lake for hours before the Ontario Provincial Police radioed to tell them that they had found and apprehended the boy in Whitby.

Eddie did not go back to a happier home.

And it would soon get worse. Although he was popular and did well at high school athletics, Eddie's classroom attendance and marks were dismal. When his mother died in 1929 when he was 15, he did what a lot of guys did when the Great Depression hit — he left school, went west and rode the rails.

Eddie never went hungry, though. Like most hoboes, he worked when he had to and stole when he could. But unlike the others, he had an ace in the hole. Blue-eyed, dark-haired Eddie was devilishly handsome and charming. He could always get a woman, young or old, to take care of him — at least temporarily. Although he called religion "baloney," he knew that playing the part of the true believer, especially with women, was essentially guaranteed to get him a free meal.

It worked out pretty well for him for a while, but in 1937, he got a bit too ambitious, held up a gas station and got two and a half years behind bars at the Saskatchewan Penitentiary in Prince Albert.

The timing of his release meant that he did not have to face the stigma that many people who get out of prison did. The Second World War had just started and the Canadian military was desperate for manpower. It wasn't the French Foreign Legion, but they did promise not to hold his past mistakes against him.

He did, however, lie on his application, claiming he had finished the tenth grade and that he knew how to fix motorcycles.

He was shipped to England and served his hitch there first as a motorcycle courier and then as a provost, or military policeman. But he once missed his duty and when they found him drunk, he was suspended two days' pay and demoted from sergeant to private.

Eddie married an English girl and brought her and their three kids — one of hers from a previous relationship — back with him to Toronto when the war was over.

He also brought back some war booty, including a Luger pistol he had taken from a dead German soldier in France and a Tommy gun he had bought from an American.

And, almost as soon as he got back, he landed a job as a streetcar driver on Yonge Street. Not only had he patched things up with his dad, but the old man was boasting about his boy's exploits overseas. The stories were sometimes a bit embellished, and Eddie became known around the area as having been a commando.

But the boredom of the humdrum job and family life got to Eddie, and the streetcar job only lasted a year. He worked some small-time menial jobs, but nothing resembling a career materialized.

That is, until he discovered a way to make easy money. He found his inspiration while reading a newspaper in the spring of 1950. The top story was about a Toronto man who had robbed a bank and made off with $69,000 — about 19 times the average annual wage at the time. The man was caught and since he was found to have a significant developmental disability, he was released once the money was returned.

Eddie marveled that a man like that could pull off such a job and almost get away with it. "If it's that easy to rob a bank," he later recalled for an interview with the CBC. "What the hell am I working for?"

Eddie came up with a plan. On the morning of September 9, 1949, he took his wife's makeup and tried to make himself look as different as possible, while still not arousing any undue suspicion. He even filled his cheeks with cotton balls. Never a drinker, Eddie swallowed "a couple of mouthfuls" of Irish whiskey for courage. He then walked into a Toronto branch of the Bank of Montreal, pulled his Luger and demanded the teller empty his tray into a bag and hand it to him. The teller began to stall, so Eddie threatened to shoot. The teller then complied, but caused a commotion. Eddie ran out of the bank and into a stolen car. He was fleeing for his life. The alerted bank manager had taken a revolver out of his desk and emptied all six chambers without hitting anyone. Eddie later said he heard them whiz by his head.

But he had gotten away with $3,000.

In a move that can best be described as cheeky, Eddie went not only to the same branch, but the same teller, a few days after the robbery to see how effective his disguise was. The teller didn't recognize Eddie as he handed him change for a twenty that he had stolen from the bank.

That was all the evidence Eddie needed to convince himself that bank robbery was as easy as he'd hoped it would be.

Eddie pulled a couple more successful jobs, but when another bank manager chased him into the street, almost catching him, Eddie decided he needed a partner.

He settled on Howard Gault, a former prison guard who'd fallen on hard times. He'd had some gun training and needed money badly, so Eddie took a chance on him.

On July 31, 1950, the pair relieved a Dominion Bank branch of $2,000 and a .38 revolver they had hoped to use for protection.

It had been less than a year after his first heist, but Eddie was already famous in Toronto. Of course, the media didn't know his name, but they frequently reported on the handsome, dashing bandit who always wore a fedora.

In response, Mayor Allan Lamport blasted the banks for lax security, saying that men realized they could take home a year's pay from a stickup and not really have to worry about getting caught or injured.

Perhaps feeling slighted by the mayor's remarks, the Toronto police hauled in a suspect in the July 31 robbery named Peter Marino. He was quickly convicted and thrown in jail. The cops congratulated themselves through the media for quelling the crime wave.

While the Marino conviction probably concerned Eddie, it didn't slow him down. He wanted to go back out there, but did not want to involve Gault again. The older man hadn't helped much, and he was so slow and ungainly, Eddie knew he was vulnerable to getting caught. He certainly hadn't done enough to warrant getting half the pot.

So, Eddie struck out on his own again. On October 11, 1950, he hit an Avenue Road branch of the Imperial Bank. It was commonplace back then for bank managers to have guns in their desk drawers, and when the manager of the branch, W.H.G. Smith, saw a handsome man in a fedora waiting while a frightened-looking teller poured cash into a sack, he approached the scene with his gun drawn. He warned Eddie that he'd shoot. Instead of fleeing, Eddie pulled his own gun. Both men would later say the other shot first, but neither claim was ever conclusively proven. What we do know is that both men emptied their weapons and failed to hit anyone.

Eddie got away, but he was deeply unnerved by the incident. Perhaps thinking about going straight, he applied to the City of Toronto for a job, any kind of job, and was accepted onto as a street paver with the Works Department. On his first day, he was surprised to see that Gault was on the same crew.

The job was awful. It was hard work, the asphalt was hot and it stank, and the pay was a mere $1.10 an hour.

Perhaps as a respite, he hit another bank, taking $3,000 from a Bank of Montreal branch on March 19, 1951. But he went back to work the next day and kept working until the end of July, when a careless truck driver sped by the road crew and hit Eddie.

For the rest of his life, Eddie claimed that he was unable to hold down a job after the accident. But the government turned down his compensation claim, declaring him fit for work.

No longer interested in legal work, Eddie recruited his younger brother Norman and Gault to rob a Dominion bank in Willowdale on September 1, 1951. Their disguise was simply to rub dirt on their faces and wear filthy old clothes. They made off with $8,000.

It was a successful job, but it was also another brush with danger and an object lesson. Norman had bragged about being part of the job to a friend who told the cops. Eddie's little brother was hauled in and charged, but was released after questioning due to a lack of physical evidence.

It didn't frighten Eddie off, but he never used Norman again.

On October 16, Eddie and Gault hit a Dominion Bank just south of Lawrence Avenue on Yonge Street. Their disguise this time was simply to remove their false teeth. But Eddie had no trouble being understood as he entered the branch with his gun drawn.

While he was collecting the money, he noticed that Gault was going off script. He was waving his gun around and throwing sacks of money in the air. It suddenly occurred to Eddie that his partner was drunk. He did his best to get Gault to smarten up and, in the chaos, did not see Adelene Jamieson, the manager's private secretary, crawl under her desk and trigger a silent alarm.

Upon hearing sirens, Eddie struggled to get Gault — still acting the fool — out of the bank, just as police were converging on it. The robbers, sacks of cash in hand, fled.

One cop, Frank Skelly, chased Eddie, but he managed to get away after a scuffle at the door of his stolen Chevy. Bashed by the driver's-side door, Skelly was on the pavement when Eddie peeled out. When he got back up, the officer drew his service revolver and shot at the car, but didn't manage to hit it.

A motorcycle cop, Walter Maclean, chased after Gault. The big man had already dropped his revolver and a bag with $12,000 in it. Maclean stopped his bike and squeezed off two warning shots.

The winded fat man finally made a smart decision, stopped running and put his hands up.

Eddie had been meticulous. He had even stolen plates from another car to put on the car he stole. But there was nothing he could do about a guy like Gault. Before they even got him in the squad car, Gault had given up everything he knew about Eddie — his name, address, family members, even the make, model, color and year of his pickup truck.

Eddie didn't know that when he stashed the stolen Chevy and raced for home in his truck. A police car pulled up alongside him as he drove down York Mills Road and the cop in the passenger seat lowered his window and aimed a gun at Eddie's head. That worked far better than any lights or siren ever could, and Eddie pulled over. He warned them about the Luger before he exited the truck, then gave himself up quietly.

Eddie later claimed that the cops slapped him around while getting his confession, but they denied it. Either way, he owned up to a series of bank robberies and was sent to the notorious Don Jail — which, 23 years earlier, had been compared to "the Black Hole of Calcutta" by a Toronto grand jury, and had only gotten worse.

Eddie later maintained that he'd plan to go straight at that point, but he was prevented by two guys he met inside. Leonard "Tough Lennie" Jackson and Willie "the Clown" Jackson, no relation, were a pair of career criminals held in cells near Eddie's and quickly became his friends. Eddie and Lennie were awaiting trial, and Willie was facing a seven-year stretch in Kingston for armed robbery with violence.

Lennie had been a combat soldier in the Second World War and told people he had left a foot behind in France. In reality, his left foot had been crushed by a freight car he was trying to hop, and had to be amputated.

But it was his ace in the hole. He used his artificial foot to smuggle a couple of hacksaw blades into the Don. He recruited Eddie and Willie to tie sheets together to make rope. He then cut the bars to a window, the three men slipped out and used their rope to scale the wall. On November 4, 1951, Eddie and the two Jacksons escaped from the Don Jail.

Lennie had arranged with his sister's boyfriend, Steve Suchan, for a ride, but Suchan had forgotten and wasn't there. Rather than wait, the gang ran up the partially wooded Don Valley toward the house Suchan shared with Lennie's sister.

The cops combed the area, but could not find the escaped men. The following day, they released a wanted poster with pictures and descriptions of all four men and the offer of a $500 reward.

Lennie hid out with his model girlfriend, Ann Roberts, while Eddie and Willie went to a rooming house owned by Suchan's parents.

The boredom got to them from time to time, and Eddie and Willie would often take trips downtown, just for a little excitement. Although he said it was so he wouldn't be recognized, Eddie added a little more excitement to the evenings out my invariably wearing women's clothing and makeup. Willie later said that Eddie was delighted that he could walk down Yonge Street with everyone believing he was actually a woman.

The gang ramped the excitement up even further when Eddie, Suchan and both Jacksons hit a Bank of Montreal for $4,000. Witnesses recognized them from the wanted poster, and the media went wild. Led by Toronto Star reporter Jocko Thomas, they ran story after story about the Boyd Gang, each wilder than the last. But they, particularly Thomas, made some mistakes. He later said he named "them the Boyd Gang" because "they were led by the master bank-robber Alonzo Boyd." While Eddie might have been the interesting one, he was not the leader — Lennie was — and Eddie did not go by the name Alonzo as an adult.

But the gang did live up to their fame. Later in November, they held up the Royal Bank's Leaside branch. Lennie knew that most people in the area cashed paycheques on Friday evening, so he decided to hit the bank Friday morning when it was full of cash. He could not have been more right. The bank had more than $100,000 that day, and the boys made away with $30,000 of it. It was the biggest haul in the history of Toronto bank robberies.

The media again went wild. People could not get enough of the Boyd Gang, and cheered them on like Billy the Kid or Bonnie and Clyde.

While Eddie and Willie were hiding out at the rooming house, Suchan's father, Joseph, convinced them to hide their loot in the house's floorboards, telling them that the cops would never find it even if they had managed to track them down. They agreed. But as they slept that night, Joseph Suchan took $17,000 of it and left. He was on a flight to Miami Beach before the boys woke up the following morning.

Willie found out from Suchan's mom and woke Eddie up by telling him: "We're not rich anymore; the old man took off with the money." Eddie then grabbed his gun and pointed it at Suchan's mom, shouting at her to tell him where her husband had gone. But all she could say was the truth; she didn't know.

Without much cash and with an incredible amount of heat on them from the cops and media, the Boyd Gang fled to Montreal. Things settled down for them there. Lennie and Roberts got married, and left for Winnipeg to celebrate their honeymoon.

But without his steadying influence, things started to go awry. Willie made the mistake of letting someone see the revolver in his waistband when he drunkenly navigated his way into a nightclub restroom. The concerned man called police, who arrested him without incident. They were more than happy to find that they not only had a bank robber in their custody, but a famous jailbreaker too. Without delay, he was sent to Kingston.

Deciding that Montreal was probably less safe for them than Toronto, Eddie and Suchan returned to Toronto. Once there, they hit another bank. This time getting $10,000.

On his next job, in March 1952, he took two new guys into a downtown Toronto Bank of Montreal and made off with $24,000.

The cops in Toronto were working overtime to quell the bank robbery epidemic, and the return of what the papers called the Boyd Gang meant that more money would be lost and more bank managers would be taking pot shots at crooks, putting everyone in grave danger. One of their best men — Detective Sergeant Edmund Tong, who was the guy who'd put Lennie in the Don Jail in the first place — knew that the most valuable tool any cop has is informants, and he canvassed everyone he knew about the bank robbers.

One of the hundreds of tips he got led him to the gang. Tong was told to keep his eyes open for a black 1951 Mercury Monarch downtown. He and his partner, Detective Sergeant Ray Perry, saw one on College near Landsdowne on the morning of March 6, 1952 and drove past it in their unmarked car. Perry then made a U-turn, and pulled the car over. Tong, weapon holstered, went over to the Monarch's driver's-side window just as Perry was exiting their car. Just as Perry was approaching, he heard a loud noise, saw the Monarch's window was open and Tong on the ground. Then he felt a searing pain in his own left arm. Shots were being fired from inside the car.

The first bullet from the super-powerful .445-caliber pistol not only traveled through Tong's organs, it managed to sever his spine. Perry had been shot, and was losing blood, but managed to get back to the car and call for reinforcements. Tong was alive, slipping in and out of comas in Toronto General Hospital.

Perry identified Lennie and Suchan, and incorrectly believed that Eddie was also with them. Informants had let them know that the gang had fled back to Montreal to distance themselves from the heat.

The media reflected the change in public enthusiasm for the bank robbers after Tong was shot. Until that point, many people cheered them on — robbing banks really only hurt the banks and insurance companies — but now a good man, a family man, was near death.

Two days after Tong was shot, detectives working on informants' tips, tracked Suchan down to a fancy Montreal restaurant. They watched as he ate a lobster dinner and followed him to his apartment upstairs. When they busted in, Suchan drew his gun. But the cops already had theirs out and he was shot in the chest, arm and hip before he could pull the trigger. Inside his apartment, they found the gun that had been used to shoot Tong and Berry.

Three days later, a woman called the Montreal police and told them that she recognized Lennie from his picture in the newspaper, and that he lived in the basement apartment next door. Toronto detective Jack Gillespie, who was in town for the express purpose of tracking down the Boyd Gang, led a team of Montreal uniformed cops and detectives to the Lincoln Street address.

Gillespie knocked on the door, weapon drawn. Lennie answered, gun in hand. The two men knew each other and on recognition, started firing. Although Gillespie had managed to hit him in the belly, right hand and twice in his left arm, Tough Lennie lived up to his reputation and held the cops at bay with his two semiautomatic pistols. He also had a Tommy gun, but had not been able to assemble it without instructions. Bullets poured in from the door and two windows. Ann, pregnant, dropped to the floor, and was not hit. She pleaded with Lennie to give up while he taunted and threatened the police. Finally, when the police started lobbing in tear gas, Ann managed to convince Lennie to surrender for the baby's sake. More than 1,000 people had gathered to watch as he walked out with his hands over his head.

Despite firing dozens of bullets, Lennie hadn't been able to hit a single cop, although he did manage to injure Gillespie when a bullet hit a wall near him and a sharp bit of plaster cut him near his temple.

Lennie had been hit several times, but none of the holes in his body were life-threatening. Gillespie interrogated him on his hospital bed. Lennie told him he had no idea where Eddie was, and got seriously offended when the detective intimated that Eddie was in charge of the gang. Lennie corrected him — it was his gang. He also assured his old adversary that he'd manage to "get out" again.

Another smart Toronto cop — Detective Sergeant Adolphus Payne — couldn't believe his luck tracking Eddie. He'd seen a newspaper classified ad listing a pickup truck for sale that matched Eddie's. He sent an undercover cop Eddie didn't know to the Heath Street address given in the ad to ask about the truck. The cop recognized Eddie immediately.

Payne didn't want to see another prolonged gun battle, so he consulted the apartment building's owner, Eddie's landlord. He provided Payne with a key to the backdoor and drew him a floor plan of the building and apartment.

Before the sun came up on the morning of March 15, 1952, Payne quietly surrounded the house with 60 cops while he and two other detectives snuck in the back door. It was a Saturday, so they expected Eddie would be asleep in the master bedroom upstairs.

They crept up the stairs, making as little noise as possible. The door to the bedroom was open, Payne, who had interrogated the suspect once before, recognized Eddie in bed with his wife. Payne and one of the others tiptoed their way in, and a big cop leapt onto the bed and held Eddie down while Payne pointed his gun between his eyes. "It's Payne, you son of a bitch," he told him. "If you go for your gun, I'll blow your head off."

Eddie surrendered without incident. Payne had been wise to sneak up on his quarry. A search of the house found five loaded handguns (two within reach of the bed) and a letter to the editor of

The Toronto Star, signed by Eddie, warning the police to back off unless they wanted more cops shot.

They kept Eddie in the apartment until Lamport could arrive to pose for some pictures with the notorious bank robber.

Eddie was sent back to the Don Jail. And, after they were well enough to travel, so were Lennie and Suchan. Nobody was surprised when the guards found hacksaw blades in Lennie's artificial foot. They confiscated not just the blade but the prosthetic as well, and Lennie later fashioned a replacement out of a tin cup.

The Don Jail had been fortified since the gang's early escape and its new boss, Thomas Brand, told the newspapers it was "escape-proof."

At first, Lennie was separated from Eddie, Willie and Suchan, but when Brand's men received a tip that he was plotting an escape and the news of Tong's death on March 23 broke, Lennie was moved into the same wing because it was considered more secure.

It wasn't.

Lennie noticed that the keys the guards used were old and simple. The locks were more than a hundred years old, and worked on just three levers. With a hacksaw blade smuggled in by a lawyer, he managed to make his own key out of a spoon. After a few failed attempts, he was able to get the doors of his and his gang's cells open; and, early on the morning of September 8, they once again made it to freedom.

That unleashed pandemonium in town. An unnamed cop told the Telegram: "These men have nothing to lose. Two of them were in the shadow of the noose. They'll shoot anyone who gets in their way. There'll be a lot of killing before this is over." The first three pages of the Star reported on nothing but the escape, and it was the lead story on the first-ever CBC TV newscast, read by Lorne Greene and heavily dramatized.

Mayor Lamport suspended Brand and all seven officers on duty that day and replaced them with OPP officers. He even told the Star that the jail was "run by morons." Lamport also offered a $26,000 reward for their capture and it was reported that every cop in

Ontario had been instructed to "shoot to kill" if they spotted any of the gang.

Even with Lennie's makeshift artificial foot, they managed to make their way through the Don Valley all the way to the Yonge Street and Sheppard Avenue area, which was then mainly farmland. The cops had received a tip that the fugitives were hiding on the jail's roof and had concentrated their efforts there.

The gang hid in an abandoned barn, stealing food, until a concerned neighbor called the police, telling them that a bunch of hoboes were squatting in a barn near her house and she didn't like the look of them.

Not taking anything for granted, the police surrounded the barn and told the occupants to come out with their hands up. Lennie, Willie and Eddie gave up without a fight. When a North York cop went into the barn to search for guns, he saw Suchan on his hands and knees. The cop, Constable Ernest Southern, threatened to blow his brains out if he made a move. Suchan surrendered. The Boyd Gang was in police custody. Southern told the CBC that they all looked "pretty fed up."

Lennie and Suchan were tried for the killing of Tong and the attempted murder of Berry, even though all the evidence indicated that Suchan had done all the shooting. They were represented by Canada's most famous lawyer — J.J. Robinette, who had earlier gotten the conviction that led to Evelyn Dick's death sentence overturned. He'd heard about the case, of course, but only had a passing interest in it until one night when he was working late, one of the office cleaners asked him to represent her son. Robinette asked who her son was, and she answered that it was Suchan.

Suchan told Robinette that he had no idea Tong was a cop. He thought he was an angry driver, who he had cut off a few blocks earlier. He went on to say that his intention was to shoot the other car's engine to prevent the angry motorist from chasing him once he peeled away.

As a testament to his talent, Robinette managed to spin that story, and contemporary observers contended that he was winning jurors over to his argument that Suchan was guilty of manslaughter perhaps, but not murder.

His work was unraveled when Jackson took the stand, though. He admitted that they were on the run from the law, that they knew Tong and Berry were cops and that Suchan had shot them. When asked why he gave himself and his partner up, he replied that "those sons of bitches" (the Crown attorneys) were going to get him anyway, so he might as well own up.

It did not take the jury long to find them both guilty, and for them to be sentenced to death. Both men's lawyers appealed the convictions, but to no avail. Lennie's lawyer, Arthur Maloney, was so moved by the idea of his client's plight and contrition that he devoted much of the rest of his life to the campaign to abolish the death penalty.

Lennie and Suchan were scheduled to be hanged at 8 a.m. on December 16, 1952. But the executioner had misunderstood the instructions and arrived at the Don Jail at midnight. Unwilling to wait, he had the jailers wake the doomed men up. They were marched to the gallows — Lennie had to hop because he was denied the use of an artificial foot — and hanged simultaneously, facing away from one another, at 12:14 a.m.

Willie was given 20 years for his term with the gang and the seven from the previous conviction he had skipped out on were added. But he was paroled after 14 and faded into history.

Eddie was handed eight concurrent life terms; but, his charm never having left him, was paroled after just 10. He had been put in a lot of hard work in the prison's canvas shop, learned to weld and said he had "found God." It seems that the parole board ignored the fact that he had also twice been caught trying to saw his way through the bars on his window.

He returned to Toronto. With his wife and children estranged, he was greeted only by reporters, photographers and cops who tracked his every move.

It didn't take long before he was back in the Kingston Pen. In his four months of freedom, he had broken his release stipulations by associating with known criminals, moving without informing his parole officer of his new address and consorting with a 16-year-old girl named Adele. The 48-year-old Eddie claimed that their relationship was not romantic, but it was still in violation of the rules.

Four years later, he was released again, but this time to British Columbia under a new identity. He was instructed not to talk with the media, but he did.

In fact, he spoke with several reporters. Eddie had started a new life with a job helping people with mobility issues, and in May 1970 he married a woman who used a wheelchair that he met through his job. A few years later, the couple and another woman who also used a wheelchair moved into a house that had features that accommodated their issues. Eddie had helped design it, and told reporters that he was quite proud of himself.

He also bragged that he was in great shape and that, at 81 in 1996, he told a reporter that he'd have no problem going over the Don Jail's outer wall again.

Most of his interviews were puff pieces, full of softball questions about the good ol' days as a bank robber or about how he'd turned his life around. Journalist Brian Vallée made a documentary about Eddie, portraying him as the gentleman bank robber everyone believed him to be.

After the film, Vallée stayed in touch with Eddie and joked that he knew more about him than anyone else. Eddie responded with a chuckle that he didn't know about the killings. Vallée filed that away, and when he was researching a different story, he came across the unsolved 1948 murder of George Vigus Jr., 39, and former beauty pageant winner Iris Scott, 21, in Toronto's High Park. The pair had been strangled, and their bodies found in the trunk by Vigus's son and his friends after the police had returned the missing man's car without searching it.

Vallée started calling Eddie regularly, mixing questions about the murder and recording every call on tape. Eddie told him "I was the guilty one" when they discussed how Scott's relatives were prime suspects, said "I could hang" if the story had gotten out and frequently referred to a couple he had to "take care of."

Vallée scheduled a filmed interview with Eddie in which he would confront him point-blank about the Vigus-Scott murder, but Eddie, the gentleman bank robber, died before it could happen.

Chapter 12

A Mother's Lies

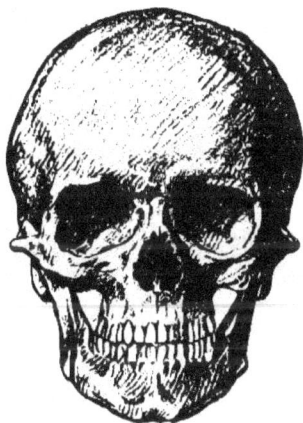

Penny Boudreau lied. When she called her new boyfriend, Vernon Macumber, from inside the Sobey's grocery store at 5:30 on the afternoon of January 27, 2008, and left a voice mail message saying that her daughter, Karissa, had gone missing and that she was worried sick, she was not telling the truth on either account.

Penny could literally see Karissa Boudreau sitting in the passenger seat of Penny's car in the parking lot of the Bridgewater Mall on the east side of Bridgewater, Nova Scotia. The car was still running so that Karissa could stay warm and listen to the radio. Just 12, she had a fondness for Disney-style pop divas like Miley Cyrus and Hilary Duff.

Not long after, at 8:35, 33-year-old Penny called the police and lied again. She told an officer at the Bridgewater Police Services' lone station that her daughter had gone missing.

She explained to the officer that when she came back to the car after buying bacon and juice in Sobey's, Karissa was gone. She also told him that she had driven to the places where her daughter would normally hang out, and driven up and down the streets of the small town looking for her, but to no avail. She lied when she said she was scared that her daughter had run away.

The officer asked if the girl had a cellphone. Penny told him that she had left it in the car.

He then asked for a description of the missing girl. She was white, with shoulder-length dark brown hair, five feet tall, 130 pounds. She was wearing jeans, a T-shirt, a black hoodie, a black vest and a pair of pink Crocs on her feet. The officer noted that her outfit, particularly the Crocs, were hardly appropriate for the wet snow they were experiencing at the time.

The cop then asked Penny to describe the events that occurred before her daughter's disappearance. She said that she hadn't really needed to go to Sobey's that evening, but took Karissa out for a ride because she wanted to have a "heart-to-heart talk" after a period of tension at home.

When the officer asked what she meant by that, she said that she and Karissa had argued about "typical teenage things," even though her daughter was just a 12-year-old in sixth grade, not old enough even for junior high school.

When Karissa did not come home that night, the police set up a media conference in which Penny, surrounded by family, made a tearful plea for Karissa to come home. She said that the two had argued and intimated that — although she had never run away before — she probably did this time. "I was trying to reach out to her as a mom and set some things straight," Penny explained on camera. She closed, tearfully, by saying: "I just want you to come home. We all love you, Karissa. I love you."

Tips came flowing in, but nothing truly useful. People in the community joined police in the search for the girl. Flyers were distributed to truck drivers and others passing through town.

Those attempts to raise awareness in the community yielded the first piece of physical evidence in the case. A man driving through Hebbville, just southwest of Bridgewater, on the afternoon of January 29, saw what appeared to be a pink shoe by the side of the road. Normally, he said, he would not have thought anything about it, but he knew that the missing girl was wearing pink Crocs when she was last seen. He stopped and checked out the shoe. It was indeed a pink Croc, women's size 8, meant for a left foot. He called the Bridgewater Police, who came and got the shoe. DNA testing indicated that it almost certainly was Karissa's. The police did not inform the public about its discovery.

Hoping that more publicity could lead to more clues, the police set up a second media conference on February 1. Penny, flanked by Macumber in an unironic wolf T-shirt, again tearfully asked Karissa or anyone who knew of her whereabouts to contact her or police.

She ended this version by saying: "It's hard to not know where your kid is."

Leanne ten Brinke, who was working towards a master's degree at nearby Dalhousie University, happened to see the broadcast. Now a PhD and one of the world's foremost authorities on lie detection, she thought something was wrong with the way Penny was handling herself. She couldn't exactly figure out what it was, but something about Penny's demeanor struck her as insincere. She then showed a video of the media conference to her faculty adviser, who agreed that something about Penny seemed evasive, like she was covering something up. But they decided not to share their opinions with police because they had nothing concrete to back it up.

The searches continued, but no clues were found. Fewer and fewer tips were coming in to police.

On February 9, a little more than a week after Penny's second television plea for her daughter to come home, a woman was driving her 9-year-old son home when he told her he had to pee. It was urgent, he told her. They were passing through Conquerall Bank, little more than a speck on the map, so she decided to stop on the gravel shoulder and let him go by the side of the highway. He was understandably shy about the whole thing, so he pressed into the woods on a trail until he found a secluded spot on an embankment on the LaHave River, away from passing traffic.

His sudden scream startled his mother, who came running. She found him sprinting back to the car. He told her he had seen toes sticking out of the snow. She followed him back to the spot and he pointed over the embankment, on the pebbly, snow-covered bank of the river, to a pile of snow with toes sticking out of it. She saw it, but wasn't sure it was what she hoped it wasn't.

Stunned, she ran back to Highway 331 and flagged down the first car that arrived. She told the driver what her boy had found, and asked him to confirm what it was. They hiked back to the site, and he, too, said that it appeared that they had discovered a dead body.

The mom called 911.

Uniformed Bridgewater police arrived, questioned the witnesses and secured the area. They did not examine the body. A Bridgewater detective and members of the RCMP's Major Crimes Unit removed the snow from on top of the body and determined that it was a white girl and, based on their own knowledge of the case, could very well be that of Karissa Boudreau.

When Matt Bowes, Nova Scotia's Chief Forensic Pathologist, arrived, he examined the body more thoroughly and determined that it had been moved to the spot before rigor mortis had set in.

From the lack of signs of struggle, he determined that the body had been dragged and dumped at the spot. Her limbs were splayed and her jeans and Winnie the Pooh underwear had been pulled down and were wrapped around her right ankle. Bowes noted ligature marks on the girl's neck, a likely cause of death and an indication of homicide. He would perform the autopsy himself, but had to wait for the frozen body to thaw.

After comparing the body with dental records, police positively identified the dead girl as Karissa Boudreau. They announced their discovery of the body to the public, but withheld specific details, including the girl's identity.

Although they did not have many physical clues, investigators began to suspect Penny. There was just something about the way she behaved that did not sync with how grieving parents acted in their experience. But they didn't have anything stronger than a hunch to go on.

Two days after the discovery, they got a little more. At about 3:20 on the afternoon of February 11, police received a call from the downstairs neighbors of Penny and Macumber's apartment at 220 Jubilee Road. The couple — who the neighbors said frequently "partied" — seemed to be fighting. There was shouting and what sounded like objects being thrown. They distinctly heard Macumber tell Penny he was going to leave her. That prompted them to listen in more intently. They told the cops they heard Macumber shout things like "Penn, how could you do this?" and "Penn, Penn, c'mon, speak Penn, how could you do this? How could you do this? I don't understand, you got me involved." They also distinctly heard him say he was "disgusted" with her.

Bowes performed the autopsy on February 13. He determined that she was a healthy girl with no injuries aside from the ligature marks on her neck. Although her pants were down on discovery, there were no signs of sexual activity. After his thorough examination, Bowes was convinced that death was caused by asphyxiation brought about by intentional strangulation. It was Bridgewater's first homicide since a stabbing in 1993.

That night, Corporal John Elliott of the RCMP's Southwest Nova Scotia Major Crime Unit called Penny and asked her and Macumber to come to the station because they had some news on the case. They arrived at 9:43 the following morning, and Elliott informed them that the body that had been found was indeed Karissa's. He gave them a moment for that to sink in, and then arrested them both for her murder.

Macumber agreed to be interrogated, while Penny exercised her right to remain silent.

Nothing Macumber said to police was much help, so they tried a different tack. Macumber was placed overnight in a holding cell with an undercover officer posing as an organized crime chieftain.

They talked, and became friendly. Although Macumber didn't tell the officer anything incriminating, the pair did establish something of a bond and the undercover cop told him that he'd like to see him after he got out, saying that he might have some high-paying work for him.

Both Macumber and Penny were released the following morning as the police did not have enough evidence to warrant charging them.

Karissa's funeral was held February 20. Her obituary stated that there was to be no visitation at the request of the deceased's mother and "loving stepfather." Donations, it said, could be made to the local SPCA.

Not long after, Macumber received a phone call from the undercover cop. They set up a meeting to discuss setting Macumber up with some work for his crime organization. Macumber agreed and they scheduled a meeting in a nearby motel for February 25.

It was the first of many meetings between the men over the next few weeks.

The police were setting a trap, using what cops call the Mr. Big Sting. In it, an undercover police officer poses as a crime boss and offers the suspect work under the condition that he or she "come clean" and admit to any crimes they had already committed. That way, the fake kingpin says, he knows he can trust his new would-be employee, and that he hasn't been involved in anything that could jeopardize the organization.

But first, they would have to gain his trust. The undercover cop sent Macumber on jobs, generally ferrying bags around town to other undercover cops, and paid him in cash.

On the same day as Macumber's first meeting with the cop posing as a crime boss, a local man stopped by the Bridgewater public pool, a five-minute walk down Jubilee Road from the apartment Penny and Macumber shared. It was one of the many places around town that he regularly checked the garbage cans in search of returnable bottles.

While searching through the trash, he came across what he described as a "pink sandal." He found it a bit odd that there would be one perfectly good shoe in the trash, and mentioned it to his fiancée when he came home that night. She had been following the Boudreau murder case and knew the girl was wearing pink Crocs when she was last seen.

The couple went back to the trash bin, and confirmed that it was a pink Croc. They called police. Officers from the Bridgewater police arrived and they determined that it was a right Croc, women's Size 8, a perfect match to the one found earlier. They also discovered a black hoodie and a black vest, both of which matched what Karissa was said to be wearing when she was last seen.

Macumber was still running jobs for the man he thought was the local godfather, and the extra cash helped him and Penny move out of Bridgewater — where they had become pariahs — to separate but nearby apartments in Halifax on April 1.

The undercover cop believed he had gained Macumber's trust; and, at an April 16 meeting, he asked him if he had committed any crimes, Macumber said he hadn't done anything major. The cop then asked him why he was in jail, wasn't it for murder? Macumber told him that he had nothing to do with Karissa's murder, that he was actually asleep when it happened. He told his new friend that he was certain that Penny had killed the girl, but she hadn't admitted as much to him. The cop, acting incredulous, asked him why he was still with a woman he thought was capable of murdering her own daughter. Macumber replied that he was simply making sure she didn't implicate him in a crime he did not commit.

The police had long suspected Penny knew more than she was letting on, but could not get her to crack even a little.

It wasn't because she wasn't under significant pressure. Neighbors and people on the street in Bridgewater wanted nothing to do with her. They ignored her when they didn't outright abuse her. She had some anonymity after relocating to Halifax, but that evaporated when local media began to speculate on the DNA evidence and released the name of her employer.

On May 3, Mr. Big told Macumber that he had a job for him to do, but he would need a female accomplice. After some initial reluctance, he was convinced to bring Penny in to talk.

Penny and the phony crime boss got along well, and he quickly gained her trust. On a May 14 meeting, he asked her how she was coping with the murder investigation and all the media attention. Penny told him how rough it was, and said that she wished the "police exhibit vault would burn down or blow up."

The cop posing as the crime boss said that if Penny played by his rules, doing everything he said, he could "make her problem go away."

She agreed.

That conversation, recorded and played back for a judge, allowed police to get a warrant to record her phone and internet communications.

It was on June 11 that Mr. Big told Penny that he needed to know if she had ever committed any major crimes. It was then that she willingly, even enthusiastically, unraveled her story.

After Penny split with Karissa's father, Paul Boudreau, to move in with Macumber, the girl first lived with her dad before moving in with them. It was not a happy situation, with constant arguments. The 12-year-old's needs did not fit into the lifestyle they preferred.

In January 2008, Macumber, she said, issued an ultimatum — either the kid goes, or he would.

On Sunday January 27, in the late afternoon, Penny invited Karissa on a car ride so they could talk. They drove all the way to Lunenburg and, while they were returning, their discussion devolved into a fight.

The undercover cop asked what happened next. Penny replied: "I did what I had to do."

She then recounted her crime as though she was describing a movie she had seen.

She left Karissa in the car when she went into Sobey's to call Macumber. She then put her groceries in the car's trunk and slipped a length of strong beige packing twine into her pocket.

Once they were back on the road and not headed straight home, Karissa kept asking to be let out of the car so she could walk back. She was tired of fighting and did not want to continue. But Penny just kept on driving until it was dark.

She went to a deserted stretch of tree-lined, unlit William Hebb Road between Bridgewater and Hebbville and stopped the car. She said to Karissa: "Okay, if you want to get out, then get out."

The girl, dressed lightly on the cold and snowy winter night did just that. She was less than a mile from home.

But Penny told Mr. Big that she just couldn't allow Karissa to "go back and tell people what a horrible mom she was."

Penny opened her own door and ran for her daughter, intending to grab her by her hood. But she slipped in the wet snow, taking them both down to the ground. Penny was on top of Karissa using her knees first on her chest and then on her arms to immobilize her. Karissa screamed "mommy, don't!" as Penny wrapped the rough, scratchy twine around the 12-year-old's little neck and pulled in a criss-cross pattern. Karissa struggled for life, and Penny even told the undercover cop that she was able to feel her daughter's hands digging at the ground. The little girl's eyes began to bulge, her tongue stuck out of her mouth and then, as she took her last breaths, she began to foam at the mouth. Karissa was dead.

Her mother then dragged her lifeless body back to the car. She tried to prop Karissa up in the passenger seat to make it look like she was sleeping, but the corpse kept sliding down, and Penny left with her daughter's body mostly on the car's floor, out of sight for people outside the car.

Without a clear plan, she instinctively drove back into Bridgewater. She stopped in the parking lot of the Tim Hortons location across from the Giant Tiger discount store to gather her thoughts.

First, she realized, she would have to get rid of the twine. She found an empty coffee cup in the parking lot and put the twine in it, replaced the cap and threw it in one of the donut shop's familiar brown-on-brown garbage cans. It was never recovered among the hundreds of other identical cups in the receptacle.

She knew she couldn't get rid of the body that easily, so she drove out of town, down Highway 331, to come up with an idea. When she came to a lonely-looking spot near Conquerall Bank, she stopped the car and turned it off. She opened the passenger door and dragged Karissa's corpse out by her left leg. As she was dragging her, the button on the girl's jeans popped open when her body got stuck on something. As Penny tugged and tugged, the jeans and underwear came off her left leg. Penny told the undercover officer that she was actually relieved when that happened because she thought that if the body was ever recovered, it would look like Karissa had been the victim of a sexual assault, taking suspicion off her.

Penny finally got her daughter's body to the embankment, and pushed it off, hoping it would roll into the river. Everyone in Bridgewater knew that plenty of kids crossed over the frozen river, and the possibility of one cracking through the ice was always present.

But the body didn't make it to the water. It got caught on some tree roots; but Penny was sure that the heavy snows that were predicted that night would hide it until the whole thing blew over.

She said that she was just about home when she noticed that Karissa's hoodie, vest and Croc were still in the car. She put them in the public pool's garbage can, and wondered briefly where the other Croc was.

Upon arriving home, she called the police, family and friends to report Karissa as missing.

While all of her story jibed with the investigation's findings, almost none of its details had been made public.

Throughout the meeting, Penny had physically re-enacted portions of her story in order to convey it more accurately to the man she believed was a criminal. She did not know that it was all being recorded on video.

As a fail-safe, the undercover cop asked Penny to write down what she just told him on a legal pad. Obligingly, she did.

He then asked why she would kill her daughter.

Penny answered that it would be harder for her to lose Macumber than it would be to lose Karissa. Forced, she believed, to choose between the two, she picked Macumber.

The cop wasn't finished with her yet. He asked her to show him where she committed the murder and where she dumped the body. She agreed, and gave directions as he drove her in a car that had a recording device inside. She took him first to the murder site, which also happened to be where the first pink Croc was found, and then to the dumping site, which was where the little boy found the body, calmly recounting and re-enacting her actions of that night all the while.

The undercover cop drove her home to Halifax, and waited in the car while she retrieved a sweatshirt she had been wearing on the night of the murder.

Three days later, Penny was arrested at her Halifax home. She was interrogated by members of the RCMP's Truth Verification Section, but again would not crack.

That is, until they showed her the video of her conversation with their undercover officer. Witnesses described seeing her smile leaving as her face instantly went pale. Within minutes, she provided the police with a detailed written confession under the condition that she also be permitted to write a letter of apology to Karissa.

After consulting with an attorney, Penny pleaded guilty to second-degree murder and was sentenced to life in prison without the possibility of parole for 20 years. The Crown accepted the lesser charge to save the community from "the anguish of a trial."

Her court appearances always drew protesters who called her "child killer" and "murderer."

Macumber was not charged. "Our understanding was that he indicated to her: 'We have to do something within our family, you have to either choose her or me,'" Crown attorney Paul Scovill told reporters outside the courthouse. "We were satisfied he did not mean that she was to kill Karissa."

For his part, Macumber said he issued the ultimatum because he came home every day to find Penny and Karissa screaming at one another. He expected that Karissa would go live with her father or grandparents or some other relative.

Macumber said that the period after the murder were hard on him as family, friends and co-workers turned their backs on him and strangers confronted him in the street. "I had no idea it would be the last time I'd see her. I had no idea," he told CTV News. "I think about her all the time, though. There's not a day goes by that I don't think of her."

Even as the years pass, mentions of Penny on social media still draw outrage. Reports that she is serving her sentence in a relatively comfortable minimum-security facility and that she has frequent interaction with children have elicited angry responses and calls for her to "burn in hell."

Chapter 13

The Boy Next Door

Sean Hine didn't want to go home, but he knew he had to. He'd spent the day at his girlfriend's place burning CDs and playing pool and generally having a good time. But it was getting late on a Tuesday night — August 16, 2005 — and he had to drive back to his own place in Richmond Hill to get ready for work the next day.

When it was almost time for him to go, Alicia Heather Ross — the girl he had been seeing for almost two months — said she'd walk him to his car. But she wanted to say good night to her mom, Sharon Fortis, before he left. So at about eleven, Alicia ran upstairs to say good night to Sharon — who, along with husband Julius, adopted Alicia when she was still just a baby.

Upon seeing her daughter bound up the stairs, Sharon paused the movie she had been watching, said good night to Alicia, and went to bed uncharacteristically early.

Alicia lived in the basement of the family's big Thornhill home. It had to be big, because it was always packed. Sharon and Julius, had six kids (although two were away at school at the time) and always had dogs. The family had a fondness for standard poodles, big dogs that require a lot of attention, care and room.

A little more room appeared as though it might be opening in the house soon, however. Alicia was 25 and doing quite well for herself. She had a good steady job with Computer Impact Marketing doing contract work for Hewlett-Packard and had recently been told that she was going to receive a promotion. Besides, she and Sean had been getting very close. It was starting to feel like the 29-year-old sales rep for Tiger Direct was becoming part of the family.

Alicia's apartment had a separate entrance to the outside, so at about midnight, she walked Sean out to the driveway and watched as he got into his car. He then drove back to the townhouse he shared with his brother and a friend.

The last thing Sean said before he left was "I love you."

While Sean was driving home, he called Alicia on her cellphone. She didn't answer. That disturbed him a little. Although it was a Tuesday night, it still seemed awfully early for her to have gone to sleep, considering the fact that he was just talking with her a few minutes earlier. Disappointed, Sean kept driving.

The following morning, he called her cellphone again, And again. And again. No answer. Finally, sure she'd be a at work by ten in the morning, he called her direct line at Computer Impact Marketing. No answer. He tried again, no answer. Then he tried the company's switchboard and asked for her. They told him that she had not shown up for work that morning. Nor had she called in sick.

In a panic, he called 911. Then he called Alicia's parents, who were both at work.

When they arrived, their normally quiet, almost secluded, street was illuminated with the blinding flash from dozens of cop cars, and they were greeted by several York Regional Police officers, both uniformed and plain clothes, some of whom were already inside their house.

Alicia's bright blue Toyota Corolla was still in the driveway. It was clear she had not gone to work that morning. A search of Alicia's basement apartment showed that she had left behind her cellphone, her purse, her cigarettes and even her keys. Clearly, she had not intentionally gone anywhere for this long.

Her mom noticed that her clean laundry from the night before was still piled on her bed and that the bed was still made underneath it. It was obvious to her that Alicia had not slept in her bed that night.

But she also noticed her daughter's rings placed on the back of the sink. Sharon knew that Alicia always took off her rings to wash up for bed. That made it clear to her that whatever had caused her daughter's disappearance had happened after she had gotten ready for bed, but before she had gotten into it.

In the backyard were Alicia's shoes, a drinking glass, a cigarette and the back gate — leading to Maple Valley Park and its wooded ravine — was wide open.

Detectives questioned the family and asked for pictures. Before long, Alicia's photo was in every newspaper and on every TV newscast first in Toronto, then Ontario, then the nation. The street was flooded with police cars and media crews. Helicopters roared over the house as they and several canine units searched the woods in the ravine behind the house.

Despite a drenching rainstorm, the search went on for days.

Sharon went to the press to send a message of strength to Alicia and to plead for anyone who knew anything to call the tip line police had set up. The case went national and was even featured on the popular U.S. network TV show America's Most Wanted.

Almost as soon as the news broke that Alicia had vanished, much of the attention regarding the situation on both social and mainstream media fell on Sean. In any case in which a person vanishes or meets a tragic end, the first suspect is usually their romantic partner. Cops say that history indicates that it's a smart idea.

The fact that Sean called 911 to report her missing less than 12 hours after he had last seen her last raised a few eyebrows. So too did the fact that he called 911 before he spoke with her parents.

And Sean didn't do much to help himself, either. He didn't act the way many people thought a grieving, or at least worried, boyfriend should. He struck many as aloof and uncaring. He displayed a habit of changing the subject of every question he was asked to himself, saying things like "I'm going to need therapy when this is all over" and "I'm a wreck" even when he hadn't been asked. And when he mistakenly said "I loved her" instead of "I love her" at a televised media conference, speculation in the community that he was involved in Alicia's disappearance grew rampant.

Sean invited the media to his house to help set the record straight. "I was going to propose to her next year," he told them. "We had so much planned for the rest of the summer." He showed reporters a picture of them that he kept in a Bible. On the back, written in pen, was: "My one and only. My true love. Took me long enough but now I've found you. 7/29/05."

He certainly hadn't done himself any favors when it was revealed that he had been arrested back on August 22 for drunk driving and had even spent a night in jail afterward. Police said that the incident had no connection to Alicia's disappearance, but many people speculated on social media that it actually did.

Sean's brother and roommate, 26-year-old Chris Hine, didn't exactly endear the family to the public, either. When reporters asked him about the drunk driving arrest, he laughed it off, saying that plenty of people he knew had a few drinks before taking the wheel. When a reporter asked Chris what he knew about Alicia's disappearance, he cryptically said "I know a lot of things," and refused to speak any further on the issue.

Although the police said that Sean was a "valuable witness" and not a suspect, the media saw it differently. Toronto Sun columnist Thane Burnett, in particular, wrote articles inferring that Sean was guilty.

On August 29, the National Post ran an article that cemented the idea of Sean's guilt to many in the country. It said that Sean had stopped co-operating with the investigation, and had declined to take a polygraph test.

To many, that indicated that he was clearly a liar. People mused on social media about it, wondering aloud why he would refuse to take a lie-detector test if he was telling the truth. The reason is that polygraph testing is a lot more complicated than it seems to most people. In Canada, the results of polygraph tests are not admissible in court as evidence, and are completely voluntary. It's also important to know that polygraphs measure nervousness to indicate dishonesty; and, just as many unfeeling people can beat the test and lie with impunity, some sensitive people can fail such a test even while telling the truth. In effect, Sean had nothing to gain if he had taken the test, and plenty to lose if he had.

But as time passed, and no usable leads came in, the calls stopped coming. The police command post that had been set up in a nearby schoolyard had been taken down on September 2 so it wouldn't interfere with the kids coming back to school after Labor Day.

A week later — when Barrhaven, Ontario's 18-year-old Jennifer Teague disappeared — it seemed like the Alicia Ross case was old news. The media contacted Sharon not about how the case was going so much as to get her opinion on how a mother can cope under the strain of a missing child.

Sharon continued to use every avenue she could to plead for information on her daughter, but to no avail.

Despite hard hours of interrogation, surveillance and forensic study, the police had nothing consequential to work with. That is, until a man and his lawyer walked into a police station on September 20. The man — Alicia's 31-year-old next-door neighbor Daniel Sylvester — told police that he had accidentally killed Alicia.

"His conscience got the better of him," the lawyer, David Hobson, said. "He's feeling that the family next door needed closure. He feels that another person might have been unjustly prosecuted."

The police had actually interviewed Daniel already, but had not considered him a serious suspect. The son of celebrated and recently deceased financial planner and author Grant D. Sylvester, Daniel was a loner who kept to himself and hardly ever emerged from his family's house in daylight hours. He told investigators that he was at home watching television when Alicia disappeared, as he did every night. He also told them that while he was aware that there was a big family next door, he didn't know any of its members individually. Daniel even went so far as to tell them that until they said they were looking for Alicia, he had always thought the girl next door's name was Tricia.

Little more than a month after that interview, when he admitted to killing her, the police told him that they would need to recover the body, and he agreed to bring them to it.

He took them more than 50 miles away, to the tiny hamlet of Manilla, not far from the Kawartha resort town of Coboconk.

There, in the woods, Daniel led them to a few scattered bits of human remains. Quickly, the police charged him with the second-degree murder of Alicia Ross, pending a positive identification of the remains.

Forensic investigators combed the surrounding area, but were only able to fill two small bags with her remains. Alicia had been reduced to 11 pounds of bones and bone fragments, a section of mummified skin, a tank top and two artificial breast implants. They also found a wallet nearby, full of Daniel's identification.

Medical examiner Toby Rose, who examined her remains, positively identified them as belonging to Alicia, but said that they were too badly decomposed to determine a precise cause of death, or if Alicia had been sexually assaulted before or after her death.

Back at the York police headquarters in Newmarket, Daniel gave his account of the night on video. "Basically, I killed her — she died at my hands," he told Detective Rick McVeity. "I am responsible for the disappearance of Alicia Ross, and I am responsible for her death."

He went on to say that just after midnight, he was in the narrow walkway between his house and Alicia's (he did not say why). She came through the same corridor, presumably after saying good-bye to Sean, and was startled to see Daniel.

Indicating that she knew him, he said, she angrily asked: "What the fuck are you doing here, loser?"

Daniel said that being called a "loser" trigger a furious response in him. Daniel told the police that, fueled by rage, he walked up to Alicia and smacked her, open handed, in the face.

Shocked, he said, she grabbed his shirt to prevent herself from going down to the ground. He claimed that he then grabbed her by both shoulders and dragged her to the ground, with her kicking and clawing all the way down.

With his knee, and all of his weight on her sternum, he said he grabbed each side of her head and slammed it down on the pavement several times.

"I knew she was seriously hurt and most likely dead," he told them. "I knew that I had caused her serious bodily injury; I panicked."

He then described how he paced up and down the walkway for five or ten minutes trying to decide what to do. He considered calling an ambulance, but said he was "too scared."

He then said he dragged Alicia — unsure of whether she was alive or not — into his garage. He said that blood was still coming from her head.

Daniel then said he went inside his house to shower and change clothes. About 45 minutes later, he went back to the garage, wrapped Alicia's body up and put it in his car. He also said he packed the towels he had used to clean her and the garage floor into garbage bags and drove all of the evidence up to Manilla, where he dumped it.

When he returned, he finished cleaning the garage and the walkway; apparently without waking anyone in either house.

That would have been the easy part for Daniel. He was used to going out every night. He avoided going out in the day time, he said, because he didn't like coming into contact with other people.

But he did like to drive around town in his mother's car at night. He prided himself on being able to leave unnoticed after everyone else in the neighborhood had gone to sleep and arrive home again before they all woke up.

Bedeviled by mental and emotional problems all his life, Daniel had dropped out of high school as soon as it was legal to because he didn't like "being forced into social situations." He had never had a job or a girlfriend.

Reconstruction of what remained of the body added some credence to how Daniel had described Alicia's last minutes.

Forensic examiner Katherine Gruspier had discovered more than 30 fractures in her remaining bones, mainly along Alicia's sternum and ribcage, indicating a traumatic collapse exactly where Daniel had said he had kneeled on her. But the magnitude of the injuries seemed hardly consistent with a simple knee to the chest. "We most often see these injuries when they present at the coroner's office as the result of fatal motor vehicle accidents," she said, adding that she had seen similar injuries in soldiers killed in action and people who had died in airline crashes. She pointed out that this severity of injury is rare in cases of assault because of the massive amount of force required to break a ribcage from the front. "As a structure, it's built to withstand a lot of pressure, to give before it breaks," Gruspier said. 'Something has to give with the pressure — what's going to give first are the bones."

The injuries to Alicia's face, she maintained, were unlikely to have been caused by the single slap Daniel said he had delivered before sending her to the ground. In fact, she had suffered a broken cheekbone, two broken nasal bones, two fractured neck vertebrae and a chipped tooth, all likely before she hit the pavement.

And all of Daniel's statements about their encounter ran counter to the established reality that Alicia was a big, strong person who had been trained in karate.

While Daniel seemed remarkably calm telling McVeity that he killed his next-door neighbor, he became visibly upset two days later at another taped interview. When the detective suggested that semen had been found at the dump scene, Daniel acknowledged that it was probably his. "I didn't rape her or anything like that," he nervously asserted. "I didn't fondle her, I didn't do anything in a sexual manner, I didn't have sex with the body."

Then why was there semen there, his semen, asked McVeity.

Shaking and talking quickly and in a higher pitch, Daniel admitted that he masturbated at the dump site, but only to calm himself down. "I started getting the tingling feeling, the burning feeling of panic setting in and telling myself 'It was going to be okay, I wasn't going to do it,'" he said. "So in order to alleviate the panic, I tried to … you know … calm down — I masturbated."

If there was any semen on the body, he maintained, it was only because the clothes he was wearing when he masturbated came into contact with the body while he was disposing of them both.

McVeity asked if Alicia was nude at the time. Daniel admitted that he had taken her clothes off in his garage because "they were ripped."

The detective asked him about some night-vision goggles he had owned, and Daniel bristled, claiming he had never used them to spy on Alicia.

News of charges against Daniel shocked the media. The Toronto Sun, which had been particularly vociferous in calling for Sean's head, actually issued an apology. But it was, at best, lukewarm and it appeared to try to distance the Sun from any blame. It began with the words "Admit it. You figured he did it," and blamed not the Sun or any individual writer, but rather a "presumptuous public."

Daniel's defense team attempted to have the second-degree murder charge reduced to manslaughter, but the Crown rejected the offer.

His trial pitted Daniel's defense lawyers — who claimed he had accidentally killed his neighbor in an argument — against the Crown — who maintained he murdered and sexually assaulted Alicia and then came up with a carefully crafted and much-rehearsed story to exonerate himself.

The Crown portrayed Daniel as a sinister character, a voluntary shut-in who spent his days spying on neighbors and obsessively masturbating.

His defense countered that Daniel was mentally ill, incapable of traditional social activity and flew into a reflexive, uncontrolled rage when Alicia called him a "loser."

Plenty of what little physical evidence was available was at odds with Daniel's story.

One of the primary sticking points centered around an automatic, motion-sensor controlled light on the Sylvester house that illuminated the walkway between the houses. The forensics team determined that the light was in working order on the night of the killing, and could be controlled from inside the Sylvester house.

The Crown argued that if the light was off, it was likely that Daniel had turned it off so that he could attack Alicia under the cover of darkness.

It was impossible to determine whether the light was on or not scientifically. The court would have to rely on eyewitness testimony, and the only other person who had been in the walkway after dark had been Sean.

When he was initially questioned by police, Sean said that the light had been on, which supported the defense. But at the trial —

Sean testified via video link from a courthouse in Florida, near where he had relocated and started a new life with another woman — he testified that the light was off when he left the house.

That testimony was damning to Daniel's defense. His lawyer, Hobson, accused Sean of lying under oath. He said that he believed that Sean changed his story to support the Crown's case in hopes that the police would make a deal with him regarding his drunk driving charge.

Sean became flustered, and had no explanation for why he changed his story regarding the light.

Hobson pointed out that if Daniel had not confessed to killing Alicia, it was very likely that Sean would have been charged with murder. "My client saved your bacon," he said. "How could you be so callous as to turn around and try to sink him with this evidence that was concocted?"

"That's a tough question," Sean said from Florida. "I was just trying to do what I thought was right."

Since forensic examiners found no trace of blood or other signs of struggle at the place in the walkway where Daniel said he killed Alicia, but had found no lack of it in his garage, the Crown argued that Daniel had dragged her alive into his garage, immobilized her with duct tape, sexually assaulted her and then killed her. They also pointed out that Daniel had visited the body several times. They claimed he did so to masturbate in its presence.

On May 28, 2007, Daniel was found guilty of second-degree murder. The jury deliberated for just seven hours.

"This verdict now helps all of us move forward to the day when we hope memories will be of cherished happy times rather than painful reminders of Alicia's death," Sharon told reporters.

At Daniel's sentencing hearing on July 5, Justice Edwin Minden condemned him for a "brutal, vicious and sustained attack on a defenseless and vulnerable young woman." He also said that Daniel had not turned himself in because of his conscience; but, rather, because it was only a matter of time before the body, his semen and the wallet he had accidentally left behind on one his more than a dozen subsequent visits to the dump site would be found. The jury never heard about the wallet, which Daniel admitted he lost on one of his frequent visits to the body, which he said were "just to see that it was still there."

Citing a lack of faith in the accuracy of Daniel's recounting of events, Minden said: "The grim reality is that we may never know the precise circumstances of her death."

Daniel was sentenced to life in prison without a chance at parole for 16 years.

Sean stood trial for his drunk driving arrest.

Chapter 14

Luka Magnotta, Famous At Last

E ric Newman wasn't famous, and that bothered him. He wanted to be a fashion model, but it wasn't quite working out for him. He couldn't understand why — everyone had always complimented him on his looks, and he never had a problem getting dates — but his career just wasn't taking off.

He'd been in a few semi-professional porn videos, but he knew that they'd hire anyone who'd take their clothes off in front of a camera. While waiting for his big break, he supported himself by stripping and working as a prostitute.

He did get one legitimate modeling gig, though. He posed, shirtless and pouting, for a shoot for fab, a free magazine intended for the Toronto-area LGBQT community. The bio that came with the photos was fanciful, and used an assumed name:

"This 22-year-old soccer fan was born in Russia and currently lives in Toronto. He hopes to train to become a police officer. 'I don't want to do traffic tickets. I am thinking vice or homicide.' Jimmy likes men and women in uniforms. He says his best attribute is 'my package. I got a mean dick. Me and my buddies made a few videos.' Jimmy has also been a model for Sears, sporting 'pyjamas, jeans, sweaters.' When it comes to pizza, he prefers 'Greek style with feta cheese and black juicy olives.' His email is stunningstud21@hotmail.com.

He wasn't from Russia. He'd been born on September 24, 1982 in Scarborough, Ontario. A few years later, his family moved to the tiny cottage-country village of Bethany.

Eric and his two younger siblings were home schooled by their mother, Anna Yourkin. Donald, his father, later recalled it as a "terrible" experience because their "germaphobe" mother would not let them come into any contact with any other children. Eric would later write on a blog that his mother kept him in diapers until he was seven.

In 1993, the Newman family ran into severe financial difficulties — Donald said it was because Anna had secretly charged up their credit cards to their limits and not paid — and were forced to move in with Donald's parents back in Scarborough.

Eric attended public school for the first time, enrolling in Charlottetown Junior School for sixth grade. His classmates would later recall that Eric lied constantly, telling them wild stories about his family's wealth and importance, even though they were clearly not true.

That year, his parents' marriage broke down and they divorced. Anna moved in with a man named Leo, who — Donald claimed — was abusive to the children and frequently called Eric "faggot."

After much lobbying, Anna's mother, Phyllis Yourkin, took custody of the children and moved them to her house in Peterborough and then Lindsay. Media described Phyllis as "domineering." They said that she was particularly tough on Eric, who had what some called a "submissive personality." He would later write about his time there in social media, complaining about his "absentee parents," and about how he "desperately wanted and needed" them.

He attended I. E. Weldon Secondary School in Lindsay, and classmates recalled that he was best known for changing his hair color — from black to bleached blond — frequently. He dropped out after eleventh grade. Several classmates also said that he was a frequent target for bullies, and was beaten up many times.

When he was 18 in 2001, Eric went to the emergency room at Ross Memorial Hospital, complaining of a sore throat. When he was examined, however, he told the doctor he was hearing voices. After two subsequent visits — including one in which he admitted to swallowing an entire bottle of sedatives — he was diagnosed as schizophrenic and prescribed drugs. Eric would then apply for a disability allowance from the Ontario government, which granted him $1,000 per month. He was also given a room at Harrison House, a group home for young people with mental health issues.

Unhappy there, he started visiting Toronto. Cruising the gay clubs, he is said to have met Nina Arsenault, who had recently undergone gender reassignment surgery. She said she arranged for Eric — who had started introducing himself as Luka or Rocco — to strip at several clubs, including Remington's on Yonge Street, and she said they dated for a while.

Nina later recalled to reporters that Eric was deeply troubled. He had a habit of punching himself in the face and she called him a "manipulative liar." She did say that one thing that he said to her stuck, though: "I'm afraid that when you look into my eyes … that you will see nothing inside of me."

It should be noted that several people have claimed on social media that Nina's recollections are fabrications she made after the fact to draw attention to herself. They say that Eric just started hanging around at the clubs and was asked by managers if he wanted to get up on stage.

Donald, who had been diagnosed with schizophrenia and bi-polar disorder himself, was worried about his son, and suggested he see a psychiatrist.

Eric visited Thuraisamy Sooriabalan, who checked him into a hospital briefly. Sooriabalan acknowledged Eric's schizophrenia and sent him back to Harrison House. Eric complained to his psychiatrist that the other residents there don't like him because "I am going to be a celebrity, a superstar."

Back in Lindsay, Erik — now going by the name Luka full-time — visited Allan Tan, the Yourkin family doctor, complaining of weight loss and erectile dysfunction. Tan ran an STD test, gave him a prescription for his erectile problem and gave him some advice on healthier lifestyles. Tan would later treat his mental-health problems with valium and three bouts of hospitalization.

It was about that time that Luka appeared in his first porn video, Street Bait 996:Luka. It didn't give him the stardom he expected.

Jeff Vanzetti, owner and webmaster of IAFD.com, a definitive database of adult films and performers, said he had never heard of Luka, even years later. He pointed out that Street Bait was not a big-time operator in the industry and their videos were short, quickly made and available online only. Vanzetti said that Luka was not a porn star, so much as a porn participant.

He also said that such videos are commonplace and offer the participants little more than quick cash. "It's easy money," he said of the industry. "So, if you're a guy who doesn't mind having sex on camera with other guys, it's certainly easy enough to say 'You know what, I need a couple grand, let me go do a web scene for somebody.'"

But Luka was convinced it was the first step on the road to international stardom, so he moved into a room in a Toronto family home and pursued his modelling career, although most of his income came from prostitution.

He regularly visited Sooriabalan, complaining about stress and hearing voices. The doctor ordered a CT scan, which came back negative. Luka assured Sooriabalan that he was on the road to recovery since he had joined the Church of Scientology, and found meaning in his life.

But it wasn't long after that, that Luka was charged with credit card fraud, racking up $16,900 in charges on cards that did not belong to him.

The fab shoot in January 2005 did not make him a star, either, but it did kick-start interest in his porn career. In quick succession, he made three low-level, straight to online videos — His First Huge Cock: Luka, His First Huge Cock: Jimmy and BadPuppy.com:Luka.

His health problems persisted, and he saw Tan several times. He told Tan that he believed people 23re following him and that his enemies were putting pictures of him online to sabotage his modelling career. Tan noted that Luka was frantic and delusional, but since he did not appear to be suicidal, he took no further action.

With his fraud trial looming, Luka's mother wrote a letter to Sooriabalan, asking him to write to Luka's lawyer, Peter B. Scully, to let him know about her son's mental health issues. He did, telling Scully that Luka had been diagnosed with paranoid schizophrenia and that he had been hospitalized twice after failing to take his pills.

Scully got to know Luka, who he knew as Eric, and said he didn't find him all that odd. "I've had lots of creepy characters," he said. "And Eric did not stand out as one of them." Instead, he was worried that the victim's father, who was a prominent businessman and influential in the Greek-Canadian community, or one of his friends might attempt to harm Luka, so he wrote a letter to police advising them of the situation.

The details of the fraud came out at the trial. Luka had met a young woman while chatting online. He had befriended the 21-year-old — whose doctor claimed had the mental capacity of an 8- to 12-year-old — and convinced her to get credit cards from retailers The Brick, 2001 Audio Video and Sears. He told her that he wasn't able to get credit himself because of some mix up, but would use the cards and pay the bills. Using the information he got from the cards, Luka posed as her on a telephone call to American Express and received one of their cards as well.

He racked up more than $10,000 on the retailer credit cards before the girl's mother happened upon one of the bills and got her daughter to own up to what was going on.

Luka pleaded guilty to fraud in exchange for having several other charges — including one of sexual assault against the girl — dropped. "I know you have your own problems," Judge Lauren Marshall told him, "but it is a terrible thing to take advantage of somebody with even bigger problems than you have."

Along with his 16 days of pre-trial custody, he was sentenced to 100 hours of community service (later reduced to 20), a nine-month conditional sentence and 12 months of probation. He was also ordered to take his medication regularly and advised to listen to his parents.

He did not. Luka moved from house to house and asked Tan if he could refer him to a new psychiatrist because he believed Sooriabalan was telling his secrets to his parents.

He went back to dancing at nightclubs and moved into a nearby high-rise with a roommate named Nader Eid. He introduced Luka to a performer named Barbie Swallows, and the two started dating. Barbie, who had also undergone gender-reassignment surgery, told the Daily Mail that on their first date, she joked: "I hope you aren't going to kill me or rape me, Luka just giggled."

Barbie said that she found Luka a bit creepy and aggressive and was considering breaking it off with him, but he would always try hard to win her over. "He called me one night and said he wanted to take me out to dinner," she recalled. "I said no because I wasn't sure about him, but then he turned up in a limo. I had never really travelled in a limo before. I thought that was pretty romantic."

But it wouldn't last. Barbie said she just found him to be too prone to fits of anger, and she was not comfortable with his obsessions, which included Canadian sex killers Paul Bernardo and Karla Homolka.

Luka then appeared in another porn video, called Adorable.

A few days later, he had his name legally changed to Luka Rocco Magnotta.

He visited Tan to help him with a hair transplant that had gone wrong and again complained of erectile dysfunction. Tan asked him why he changed his name and Luka told him it was because he was being followed. He told Sooriabalan the same thing.

His picture appeared in print again, but it wasn't a paid gig. Fab Boy was a magazine that linked LGBQT people for dating, and Luka's ad was featured. He said that he was looking for a "loyal man" and complained that "you can't enjoy yourself in porn videos, there are too many people around!"

Just three months after changing his name, Luka declared bankruptcy. Citing "illness, lack of employment and insufficient income to pay off debts," he was placed under bankruptcy protection. He was discharged from bankruptcy nine months later in December 2007.

His luck changed a bit a few weeks later when he was interviewed by Naked News — a Toronto-based subscription TV program on which the hosts take their clothes off while presenting the news — about his life as an escort. With slicked-back black hair and a black sleeveless T-shirt, Luka tells the interviewer in a thick Ontario accent how the sex-for-hire business works in Toronto.

He then auditioned for COVERguy, a game show in which aspiring models compete for $1,000, a fashion photoshoot, a one-year membership to a fitness club and the front cover of abOUT magazine. Now sporting blond hair, Luka told the interviewers that he wanted to win so that he could afford more plastic surgery. Although Nina Arsenault was one of the judges, she did not acknowledge him as an acquaintance. Luka was not chosen for the show.

On August 21, 2007, a distraught Luka told Sooriabalan that people had been spreading a rumor that he was dating Karla Homolka. Luka didn't know it at the time, but Homolka had relocated to the Caribbean by then and was married with children.

Whether he was deluded or not, Luka started and spread the rumor of his alleged romantic entanglement with Homolka. Several posts on forums and message boards under a number of different aliases alleging or denying the existence of a relationship between the pair have all been tracked back to Luka. He even went so far as to edit Homolka's Wikipedia page to include himself as her husband.

At the time, any mention of Homolka drew interest from the mainstream media, and several outlets reached out to Luka for comment.

In an interview for AM 640 talk radio, Luka denied he was having an affair with Homolka, and called out to whomever was spreading the rumors to stop. "I have lost modelling jobs and have been receiving death threats," he said. A similarly themed front-page article in the Toronto Sun ran with the headline "Homolka Rumour Ruins Model's Life."

But the Homolka hoax isn't the only online project Luka pursued. He used several of his identities to complain about and try to start a movement to cancel the TV show Family Guy. It drew great criticism from the show's fans on social media.

He also made a Wikipedia entry about himself, but it was deleted by admins because his accomplishments in porn videos had not made him, in their judgement, a celebrity.

In February 2008, he auditioned for another TV competition show, Plastic Makes Perfect. In his 20-minute interview, he admitted that he didn't believe people who complimented him on his appearance and that hid family didn't want anything to do with him anymore. He was not chosen to be on the show.

The following year, he appeared in another porn video, this one called Monster Cock Jocks 25.

A few weeks later, in May 2009, Luka created the first of his more than 70 Facebook identities. Luka used those fake accounts to post about himself in the third person, alleging a relationship with Homolka and referring to himself as a "celebrity model."

He also started a blog on estrip.org. In his 44 entries, he mainly wrote about how the life of a model is much tougher than most people think it is.

But he also began to think about changing careers. He enrolled in Orea Real Estate College in hopes of becoming a realtor. To deal with the stress of college, he switched psychiatrists, to Robert Weinstein, who also diagnosed him as a paranoid schizophrenic. He told Weinstein that his life changed when he was 19, because he had a boyfriend who would write "I love you" on his door in his own blood. He also told him that his boyfriend paid his rent in exchange for sex.

Less than a year later, in August 2010, Luka told Weinstein that he had to give up his courses due to stress and because an ex was harassing him. Weinstein, who noted Luka had lost a considerable amount of weight, suspected he had stopped taking his medicine, and advised him to restart.

Days later, Luka made his final porn video, Daddy Mugs Fucks Justin 2. His co-star is significantly older than him, even though Luka had said in his Plastic Makes Perfect audition that older guys were "disgusting."

He then turned the camera on himself, not for sex videos, but something more disturbing. He made three videos in which he tortured and killed kittens.

The first was Bathtime LOL in which a kitten tied to a broomstick is repeatedly lowered into a bathtub full of water until it drowns. It was uploaded to YouTube on December 2, 2010, by an account named Jasminethecat666.

Using the name Uonlywish500, he uploaded 1 Boy 2 Kittens to YouTube on December 21, 2010; its title inspired by the notorious 2007 viral video 2 Girls 1 Cup. In 1 Boy 2 Kittens, he smothered two kittens by placing them in a transparent plastic vacuum cleaner bag, then sucking the air out.

And finally, he made Python Christmas (also known as 1 Cat 1 Christmas). In it, he brings a kitten wearing Santa hat to a 16-foot python, and watches as it is devoured while The Little Drummer Boy plays in the background. It was uploaded to Flix in December 2011, with a notation that said it was recorded in Islington, England. On the same day it was posted to LiveLeak by a Linda Collins, an account whose only other post was a video called Male Model Falsely Accused of Animal Cruelty, in reference to Luka.

He appears in all three of the videos, but made enough of an effort to obscure his face that it would be difficult for anyone to make a positive identification.

While careful, he was not thorough, and he had underestimated the power and determination of animal lovers on the internet.

Luka, using fake identities, had spread news of 1 Boy 2 Kittens on several social media sites and forums. That drew the attention of dozens of animal lovers who set up a Facebook page called For Great Justice that was dedicated to revealing the identity of who they called the "Vacuum Kitten Killer."

It rapidly drew hundreds of members, many of who contributed their expertise in tracking down clues.

Quickly, members identified the brands of the blanket and the vacuum cleaner bag shown in 1 Boy 2 Kittens, narrowing down the video's geographic location. They also determined that the Russian accent used by the perpetrator was not authentic.

But ineffectual tips and false accusations flooded the page and select members moved their conversation to a private page called Useful Individuals.

They pored over the video, and others like it. They discovered a photo on 4chan of a man, face obscured, lying on the same bed and the same blanket in the video, with two kittens in his hands.

They had focused their investigation on a Facebook user who went by the name Jamsey Cramsalot Inhisass. While they were interviewing him via Facebook messenger, one of their members received an email from an account with the name Beverly Kent that read: "The name of the kitten vacummer you are looking for is Luka Magnotta." It inaccurately said that Luka was living in West Hollywood at the time.

The investigators then researched Magnotta. One of the first posts they saw was an ad on a BDSM forum, on which he wrote:

"Hey, im an extremely attractive man in my 20's, I am looking for a dom master who will be able to teach me a lesson I will never forget. I enjoy being brutally anal raped (by 1 or more men) I enjoy being forced to drink piss and eat shit, I also like to get punched and kicked until I cant move. So the bigger you are the better. I dont want any pussies or losers who will back out.. you have to be very agressive and have a strong perverted side like me. I also like to be handcuffed and driver to remote locations then thrown out in the dark so I dont know where I am (if you prefer me naked thats cool) Then we can talk about what happened when I get home and laugh hah ahaha. I love to get drunk and when I am so drunk I cant stand then you will have COMPLETE control over me, I have a hot little ass thats just waiting to get violated. message me if your serious, no time for time wasters."

They found many mentions of him online, but almost all of them were from untraceable social media accounts, often with no other posts — what many internet users call "throwaway" or "sock puppet" accounts, that are used to retain anonymity. One post from a throwaway account on a River Phoenix fansite read "I saw something tonight on You Tube where someone had stated that River and Luka were cousins?? Is this so??," one on Flickr read "Luka Magnotta arrested in New Mexico for Trying to Gain Access to Area 51 says local authoritys" and one on Facebook opened with "This is a fanpage I made for Luka Magnotta, my new idol."

After gathering what little information there was about him from legitimate media sources, they determined that the best way to catch him would be to offer him a part in a high-budget porn movie. One of the activists knew porn star Ron Jeremy, who was used as bait. But Jeremy, aware that he might have to spend time alone with Magnotta and being very much of the opinion that people who torture and kill defenseless animals are also likely to want to harm people, chickened out.

Undaunted, the group's leaders published an article on the site of Negotiation Is Over, an animal-activist group, that read:

> "After an intense investigation another anonymous tip
> resulted in the positive identification of the well known
> bisexual porn star and model Luka Magnotta. Commonly
> known for drugs, wild parties, and gay clubs, his name is
> well known in Canada and the Northern United States
> regarding stories about him being involved with Karla
> Homolka, a hated 'serial' killer. Luka, 25, lives in
> Montpellier France and travels frequently between his
> home in France and TolYatti Russia."

Its inaccuracies are a testament to exactly how much Luka had distorted the truth about himself in media.

He then flew to Paris, where he posted a photo of himself with this note on Expat.com, a social network for travelers:

> "Paris is such a beautiful city and its alot of fun, Paris is
> like the New York of Europe. Just be careful because my
> husbands wallet was stolen and its pretty common there

from what im told. Also try to visit the Eifel tower at nite, its so much more beautiful. I have found love there and I wish everyone else the same, life has been so good to me! God Bless.
Luka Magnotta

He flew to Miami in January 2011, and had a panic attack at a nightclub. Police took him to Mount Sinai hospital, where he claimed someone named Manny Lopez had abused him and drugged his drink. After a physical exam, they discharged him with instructions to return if he suffered any symptoms.

Luka then went to New York City, where he contacted a lawyer named Romeo Salta looking, he said, for help because he was being harassed by animal-rights activists and abused by Manny.

Luka then relocated to Montreal. He rented an apartment in the Point St. Charles district. The building manager recalled him as an ordinary guy who spoke with a Russian accent.

After he was publicly tied to the kitten videos, though, Luka began to receive lots of attention. On one of his frequent Google searches of his own name (and assumed identities), he found out that an activist group in London was offering a £5,000 reward for information about his location. A few days later, another organization, this one in New York, offered $7,500 for the same information.

Panicked, Luka, in his fake Russian accent, told the building manager that an emergency was forcing him to move to Toronto. The guy waived the usual two months' notice because he seemed like an okay guy.

Luka lied, he actually moved to 5720 Decarie Place (Apartment 208) in Montreal's Côte-des-Neiges neighborhood not far away.

Using a photo they found on the internet of Luka standing on the balcony of a high-rise that happened to have a Petro-Canada filling station in the background, and Google Street View, the activist group in New York managed to pinpoint his location down to Etobicoke, the eastern part of Toronto. They contacted the Ontario

Society for Prevention of Cruelty to Animals, who then called the Toronto Police.

The police tracked him down to the Point St. Charles apartment, but could not get an answer on the phone number they had. So the cop called the building manager and asked about Luka. The guy told him that he'd just missed him, that Luka had moved out two weeks earlier. He didn't have a forwarding address for him, he added, but he had said that he was headed to Toronto.

Without much else, the cops dropped the investigation.

But Luka wouldn't let it drop. On December 8, 2011, he called the office of the Sun newspaper in London. The paper had run an article about the kitten videos and had listed Luka as a potential suspect. He denied any involvement with the videos and complained about being harassed by the paper. He said that he didn't want to talk to a reporter because he was too busy and wanted to keep his name out of the media. The quick-thinking receptionist took down his name and the address of the place he was staying before he hung up.

A few hours later, reporter Alex West dropped by the Fusilier Inn in Wembley, and asked about Luka. He was directed to an upstairs room. At first, Luka didn't answer, but once he did, he agreed only to speak in the doorway, not allowing West or his photographer into the room.

West said he was taken aback by Luka's appearance. He was wearing an English-style flat cap, a leather jacket and sweatpants as well as foundation and blue eye shadow.

Luka told West that he contacted the Sun because the hotel manager complained to him that he was being inundated by calls from journalists trying to get in touch with him. Luka told West that he was getting death threats and didn't want to be "hunted down and murdered."

West — pointing out that nobody from the Sun had called him — asked why people would be after him, then suggested that it might have been spurred by the rumors of him having a relationship with Homolka.

Luka demurred.

West then moved onto the kitten videos, pointing out that he had received dozens of emails from throwaway addresses the night before, all of them naming Luka as the person behind the videos.

Luka said he would not comment.

West then asked Luka if he was the person behind the videos.

Luka said his lawyer told him not to talk to the media about them.

West asked to speak with the lawyer.

Luka said he would not allow that to happen.

West then threatened to call the police.

Luka said he wouldn't talk to them either.

West pointed out that Luka wrote online — on a domain named after him and owned by him — about manipulating the media using artificial email addresses.

Luka denied writing that, and denied using email at all.

West accused Luka of trying to create a cult of personality over the internet.

Luka denied that, and said he didn't want to talk to the media because he had received "500 death threats."

West asked him why he would get death threats.

Luka said they were because of his links in the media to Homolka.

West tried to trick him into admitting to posting the videos about the cat killings.

Luka initially fell for it, but then denied it. He also denied having a YouTube channel, or posting videos to any site.

West wanted to know why people would accuse him of things he didn't do.

Luka answered that it was the work of "crazy people." He then showed West that the room he was in was not the one in the video.

West threatened to publish a story, and asked what Luka would do.

Luka asked him not to.

West again asked to talk to his lawyer.

Luka told him that he wouldn't give him his name.

West then described Luka's website and again brought up the section on media manipulation.

Luka denied everything, saying that the section on media manipulation was about how the media manipulated him, not the other way around. He then asked for evidence that he had anything to do with the kitten videos.

West then invited him out for coffee and a chat, offering him a chance to absolve himself.

Luka declined and claimed he was the victim of "criminal harassment."

West pointed out a picture in the room of Luka with two kittens that looked exactly like the ones in the 1 Boy 2 Kittens video.

Luka claimed that they were not the same kittens and that he loves animals.

West asked him why there was so much information about him on the internet.

Luka told him that people steal his pictures and write about him. He did not give a reason why.

West said that he believed that Luka put everything about himself on the internet by himself.

Luka denied that repeatedly, speaking over West's questions. He then said that he's the victim of people pretending to be him pretending not to be him.

West asked him for his name.

Luka dithered, then denied having any other name than Luka Magnotta.

West brought up the name Eric Clinton Newman.

Luka replied that Luka Magnotta is his only name, his legal name. Then he said he's never been Eric Clinton Newman.

West pointed at the cat picture again, and asked what happened to them.

Luka said he didn't want to answer, then denied that it was him in the photo.

West laughed, because it was obviously him.

Luka quickly changed his tack, saying that he was Photoshopped into the picture.

West then asked him why people would want to frame him, and again accused him of wanting to create a cult of personality on the internet.

Luka said that wasn't true, that he was avoiding the media, and pointed out that he's denying interviews.

West countered, saying that Luka was not acting like a "normal" person. He accused him of having scripted denials and no natural surprise at the accusations or questions.

Luka said that he was offended by the accusations.

West again offered him a chance to defend himself in print.

Luka declined.

The two men then exchanged pleasantries, and a frustrated West and his photographer agreed to leave.

As they were exiting the building, they watched as the hotel manager and two plain-clothes cops escorted Luka out of the building.

Sure that Luka had been arrested in connection with the kitten videos, West called a police source to follow up. He was surprised to learn that Luka had not been arrested, just evicted for non-payment of his £40 a night rent.

Two days later, the Sun received an email from an account with the name John Kilbride. That name belonged to one of the child victims of the English Moors Murderers in 1965 — a case many of Luka's acquaintances would later say fascinated him.

The message spoke about how the email's writer met a "sexy" Sun journalist. The writer obliquely admits to being the one who made the kitten videos and says that "killing is quite different than smoking … with smoking you can actually quit." It goes on to threaten to kill again, but "this time, however, the victims won't be small animals." It finishes by calling the people of London "stupid," and says of himself "getting away with all this, now thats genius."

West took the email and all the information he had on Luka to the Metropolitan Police and was referred to the Malicious Communications Unit at Islington Police Station, and they began an investigation. Not much later, they told West that since the email was sent from a server in the Netherlands and the original kitten videos were uploaded in North America, there was nothing they could do about either.

For the next few months, Luka, using aliases, showed up online frequently. Much of what he posted were sex stories and requests for information on how to sedate people without their knowing. He also posted several racist screeds on Stormfront, a Canadian white supremacist forum.

On Christmas Day 2011, he posted — using his alias cutelittlenemo1 — on a BDSM forum looking for men to "rape" him while he visits Florida.

He then started a blog in the cutelittlenemo1 name on a free server in the Netherlands, using it to publicize the kitten videos, describe his sexual desires and to defend the concept of necrophilia. One posting — Luka Magnotta: How to Completely Disappear and Never Be Found — describes how he could outwit any pursuers. Later, experts would say it did not contain any useful advice.

Back in Montreal, on April 17, 2012, he visited a clinic and was referred to a psychiatrist at The Jewish General Hospital. In his hour-long examination, Joel Paris listened as Luka told him that he was the victim of sexual abuse, that he felt a lingering emptiness and that he had attempted suicide twice. Paris did not prescribe Luka any medication, but referred him to a psychiatrist at a community health center for regular visits.

A few days later, Luka raised the stakes on his internet posts, uploading a video to YouTube called Cannibal Serial Killer - Luka Magnotta under the name Rita VanVolkenberg. It's just a slideshow of his modeling pictures over the sound of New Order's True Faith. It got several thousand views, but the number of thumbs down votes it received far outnumbered the thumbs up.

On May 15, 2012, he uploaded a video to Vimeo under the name Angela Downs. It was called 1 Lunatic 1 Ice Pick (Non Graphic) Do you know this Guy ?, and featured the image of a young man — clearly, but not definitively Luka — wearing a purple hoodie and carrying what appears to be an ice pick. It carried the tagline "We are trying to learn the identity of this guy. Do you know him?" It was then uploaded to YouTube by an account named Alexis Valoranreich.

On the same day, he posted comment s about 1 Lunatic 1 Ice Pick on several sites using several names. The posts variously claimed to have seen it on Tor (a network on the deep or dark web) or to be looking for it. The posts that allege to have seen it claim that it's a real snuff film with necrophilia and cannibalism. One post muses about the mental health of anyone who would make or post such a video.

Three days later, Luka invited a young Colombian man to stay the night in his Montreal apartment. While the man is unconscious, Luka takes photos and videos of the two of them. In one, the young visitor is bound and gagged, while Luka, armed with an electric handsaw, sits on top of him shouting "Are you OK? Are you OK?"

At 11:30 the following morning, the security camera in the lobby of Luka's building records the two of them leaving the building. The young visitor appears in the video to be unsteady on his feet, and Luka helps him keep his balance.

Luka continued his aggressive posting. Using aliases, he posted on RipOffReport and ScamInformer, warning modelling agencies not to hire Luka Magnotta.

He also posts on Craiglist's men4men section, looking for men to appear in videos.

At 9:17 on the evening of Thursday, May 24, 2012, the lobby security cameras at 5720 Decarie Boulevard recorded Luka walk in with another man who was wearing a baseball cap, cargo shorts and a distinctive yellow T-shirt.

The young man was later identified as Jun Lin, a 33-year-old student from China. He was studying business and French in hopes of becoming a permanent Quebec resident. He kept in touch with his friends back home through Weibo, a Chinese social media platform. Much of what he sent back was pedestrian — he was fond of the Smurfs and Titanic and Quebecois folk music. But he also had another account by the name of Justin Rain (a Hollywood actor best known for a small but recurring part in the Twilight movies) — on which he posted nude photos of himself — and registered a domain called homobj.com.

About four and a half hours after they arrived, at 1:48 on the morning of May 25, a call was made from Jun's phone to the Fairmont Hotel in Vancouver. Seven minutes later, another call from the phone was made to Hostelling International's Vancouver office.

Eleven minutes later, at 2:06, the cameras caught Luka exiting the building. Notably, he was wearing Jun's yellow T-shirt. He returned at 2:13 with a small white shopping bag. While waiting for the elevator, he took a moment to adjust his hairpiece while looking in a mirror.

From 2:47 until 4:02, the cameras recorded Luka's three trips to the building's garbage disposal area. In each, he dumped garbage bags into shared bins.

Luka was then captured leaving the building at 9:08. He was wearing Jun's baseball cap. Before he returned at 12:12, he was seen on other cameras buying cardboard boxes at a Jean Coutu postal outlet, exchanging Canadian currency for euros, buying white spray paint and then buying bed sheets.

He came out again at 1:09, first to carry another bag to the garbage bins and then to go back to Jean Coutu outlet to exchange the boxes he had bought earlier for bigger ones.

After he returned, at 3:39, Luka was captured one more time dumping garbage, this time wearing rubber gloves.

About an hour later, he bought tickets for a return flight to Paris on Expedia.

After another trip to the garbage bin, he ordered a pizza by phone. The delivery guy, who arrived at 5:30, would later say he seemed coherent.

Not long after, Luka was recorded at the Jean Coutu outlet mailing two large packages.

Later that evening, he — while wearing Jun's cap — takes two heavy-looking garbage bags out of the building and returns to make his tenth and eleventh trips to the garbage room. At about the same time Jun had arrived the previous evening, Luka carried a suitcase, spray painted white, out of the building. He returned two minutes later.

At some point on May 25, Mark Marek — the owner of Best Gore, a Canadian website dedicated to showing real images of violence — happened across a video on Tor called 1 Lunatic 1 Ice Pick and posted it to his site.

In it, a man in a purple hoodie with the saw in his hand is seen on top of the unconscious Colombian friend. It then segues into the same man stabbing Jun (already dead by that point) with a screwdriver he had painted silver to make it look like the ice pick used as a weapon by Sharon Stone's character in Basic Instinct. Then it shows him cutting Jun's body into pieces, committing necrophilia with the corpse and pretending to eat some of the remains. A poster from the movie Casablanca is prominent in the background, and the song True Faith — featured in Cannibal Serial Killer - Luka Magnotta and in the film American Psycho — is playing throughout.

On the following day, May 26, the camera captured Luka taking more bags out of the building and making his twelfth through sixteenth and final trip to the garbage disposal.

At 5:17, he got into a cab for Trudeau airport. It was his last time in the Decarie Boulevard apartment. He boarded Air Transat Flight 610 for Paris.

Passengers described the man in the window seat in Aisle 33 as nervous and stinking of sweat. After a number of travelers alerted the flight attendants about him, Luka was found weeping at the back of the plane. He was returned to his seat, and continued the flight without further incidents.

On arrival, he checked into the prestigious Novotel in Paris.

At about the same time, a Montana-based lawyer named Roger Renville was surfing the internet when he came across 1 Lunatic 1 Ice Pick on Best Gore.

He was so shocked by what he saw, he reported it to his local sheriff, the nearest FBI office (in Denver) and to the Miami police department, because that was where the video appeared to him to be shot. None of them were interested.

Still haunted by what he had seen, Renville went back to Best Gore and conducted his own investigation. Through comments, he was directed to other videos on the site that led him to believe the man in the video was from Toronto, so he called the Toronto police.

After he made his complaint, the person on the other end of the phone told him what he saw was fake.

Renville told him that he couldn't know that without seeing the video.

The cop told him the story didn't make any sense and asked him "why would a killer put a video of himself up on the internet?"

Frustrated, Renville asked if there was an email address he could use to send the police a link to the video. He was told there wasn't.

While in Paris, Luka texted Jean-Christophe Robert, a man he had gotten to know on Planet Romeo, a dating site, while using the alias Canadian22. Robert allowed Luka — who he described as polite and well groomed — to stay the night, but later maintained they did not have sex.

The following day, Luka checked into a less-expensive Paris hotel using a fake passport — the kind available online and sold for "novelty uses" and are legal if not used for identification in all countries except the U.S. — with the name Kirk Trammel, a reference to Catherine Trammell, Sharon Stone's character from Basic Instinct.

While he was doing that, Jun's family — who had not heard from him for three days — reported him missing.

On the following day — May 29 — Jenni Byrne, director of political operations for the Progressive Conservative Party in Ottawa opened a box that had been delivered to headquarters in that day's mail. She unwrapped the pink tissue paper it contained to find a black plastic bag. She pulled it out, describing it later as "soft" and "mushy." When Byrne got another staffer to snip the top of the bag with a pair of scissors, they were overwhelmed by a terrible odor of decay. Byrne called 911, and left the room. It contained Jun's left foot and a note on pink paper that read "Stephen Harper and Lauren Tesky know who this is. They fucked up big time." Laureen Teskey is the wife of then-Prime Minister Stephen Harper.

The Ottawa police quickly contacted Canada Post, and inspector Genevieve Benoit tracked down another package sent from the same post office that was addressed to the Liberal Party's headquarters in Ottawa. In it was Jun's left hand. It also contained a note that read: "You need to speak to Laureen Teskey and her family. Lots to hide!!"

Interestingly, the sender's name on both packages was Renée Bordelais, which shared a last name with Homolka's lawyer, Sylvie Bordelais, and her husband, Thierry Bordelais (Sylvie's brother). Homolka herself had gone by the name Leanne Bordelais after her marriage.

At about the same time, at 10 on the morning of May 29, a neighbor of Luka's Côte-des-Neiges apartment named Mike Nadeau was taking out his trash when he saw a suitcase on the street under a tree. It was beige, but he could tell someone had hastily tried to paint it white.

When he got close to it, he could tell that it had been out there for a few days at least. It looked full to him, and when he tried to move it, he found it was very heavy — it certainly wasn't full of clothes.

There was a padlock on the main zipper, but he managed to get one of the side compartments open. He immediately wished he hadn't. The stink of decay was almost strong enough to knock him down and hundreds of maggots came pouring out.

Alarmed, he ran to get a neighbor. They returned with tools, convinced that somebody had illegally disposed of a dead pet on their street.

They quickly busted the cheap padlock and opened the suitcase to reveal Jun's torso.

Stunned, the two men ran to get Eric Schorer, manager of 5720 Decarie. He called the police, who arrived three minutes later. They cordoned off the area and began interviewing potential witnesses. They left with the security tapes.

At about four that afternoon, the Montreal cops came back with still photo captures from the video cameras. They asked Schorer if he knew the man in the picture. Schorer said of course he did, and called him "strange, but not unpleasant." He forgot his name, recalled it was odd, but then remembered that he had a photocopy of his passport in his office as part of the lease agreement. The man in the picture was identified as Luka Rocco Magnotta.

Schorer took the police to Apartment 208 and let them in. Inside, they found blood-stained mattresses and other incriminating evidence. Although they were unaware of their importance at the time, they also found several items that appeared in Luka's online videos, including the outsized Casablanca poster. Inside a closet, someone had written "IF you DoNt like the ReflectioN. DoNt look in the Mirror. I DoNt Care" in red ink.

That was enough to allow the police to issue a Canada-wide alert for the arrest of Luka Magnotta for the murder of Jun Lin.

As the news of the killing seeped through the internet, a discussion on 4chan indicated that several members believed that Magnotta took part in a discussion about the killing on another forum called Mascara and Murder, even while he was on the run.

Canadian investigators determined that Luka's passport had been scanned at Trudeau airport, and issued an international arrest warrant through Interpol. He briefly made Interpol's Most Wanted list.

Perhaps realizing the heat was on in Paris, Luka booked a bus ticket to Berlin for June 1. Earlier that day — using the name William 2323 — he answered a Planet Romeo ad by a Berliner named Frank Rupert, who was looking for a roommate.

At about the same time he was getting on the Eurolines bus, Robert — having seen Luka's picture in the morning paper — told Paris police that he believed he had hosted the fugitive earlier that week.

In Berlin, he arrived at Rupert's apartment, but found that his potential roommate could not speak English or French and, since he couldn't speak German, the two actually communicated vis Google Translate on Rupert's laptop.

Rupert accepted Luka's story that he was a Parisian who had just had a messy breakup with his boyfriend and needed to put some distance in between them. Luka and Rupert shared a sofa bed for three nights, but Rupert denied they had any sexual relations as Luka was not his type.

They did get along, though, and Rupert took him out to restaurants and nightclubs, introducing him to several friends who spoke either English or French.

While he was at Rupert's, French police search Luka's second Paris hotel room, finding his return ticket to Montreal and several items that identify Kirk Trammel as Luka Rocco Magnotta.

On June 4, Luka posted a video to YouTube of himself on Rupert's couch smoking and saying "hi" to "his fans" while Madonna's La Isla Bonita plays in the background. It was uploaded by an account called ibechillin69.

Not long after, Rupert returned home from work and told Luka that it wasn't going to work out between them, and said he should probably leave. So there would be no hard feelings, he bought Luka a pre-paid cell phone and told him about some nearby internet cafés where he could search for another place to stay.

Luka walked over to the Spätkauf Internetcafe Helin in the Neukölln borough. He immediately drew the attention of some of the people there because usually only recent immigrants — mostly Turks, Arabs and Africans — ever came into the shop.

Clerk Kadir Anlayisli — a self-described "news junky" — had been browsing the internet that morning and had read about Luka. He later described Luka as "nice" and "normal" as he directed him to Cubicle 25, but as he walked back to his desk, he realized he knew that heavily made-up face from somewhere. When Luka lifted his sunglasses to browse news articles, it hit Kadir. "He's the porno killer," he thought to himself. "I'm 100 percent sure."

He quietly called police, and they arrived — heavily armed and in force — a few minutes later. When they confronted Luka, he initially denied he was the man they were looking for, but when they persisted, he said "OK, you got me" and surrendered without further incident. Police noted that he had been looking at nude pictures of himself when he was arrested.

The following day, June 5, 2012, packages arrived at two Vancouver schools — St. Georges and False Creek. One contained

Jun's right foot, the other his right hand. Luka had spent time in Vancouver, but it's not clear exactly when. The senders on those packages were listed as Logan Valentini, Homolka's sister, and Hubert Chrétien, son of former prime minister Jean Chrétien, and had their correct addresses.

Luka did not fight extradition proceedings and was flown back to Montreal on a Canadian Forces CC-150 Polaris transport. Media reported that the flight cost as much as $375,000, the government countered that it would be too risky to fly him back on a commercial carrier.

On arrival, he was placed in solitary confinement at Montreal's notorious Rivière-des-Prairies institution. He entered a plea of not guilty. He admitted his crimes, but said he was not responsible for them due to mental illness. Still, he declined a psychiatric assessment and elected for trial by judge and jury. He did not apply for bail.

On July 1 — about two weeks after Luka's return to Canada — Montreal major crimes detective Antonio Paradiso received a fax from a lawyer named Raphael Feldstein telling him that he would find what he's looking for in some tall grass near a pond in Angrignon Park.

After a sensational trial with dozens of witnesses and thousands of exhibits and eight days of deliberation, the jury of eight women and four men found Luka to be guilty on all five counts — first-degree murder, committing an indignity to a human body, publishing obscene material, criminally harassing Prime Minister Stephen Harper and other members of Parliament, and mailing obscene and/or indecent material. That automatically carried a sentence of life in prison with no chance for parole for 25 years.

Marek, who published 1 Boy 1 Ice Pick on Best Gore, was found guilty in an Edmonton court in 2016 of having published obscene material. He was given a six-month conditional sentence, the first half of which would be served under house arrest.

Since the verdict in the Magnotta case was read, media reports have come out saying the Luka is enjoying his time in the Archambault Institution, calling it a "university setting" with "pizza parties and facials." He is said to collect photos of celebrities, primarily Marilyn Monroe, and to have decorated his dorm-like room with hundreds of them. They came, he said, in the mail from his fans.

About the Author

Aldus Greene is the pseudonym for a veteran Canadian journalist who generally does not usually write about murder. Interview inquiries can be sent to themeagerpress@gmail.com.

About the Publisher

The Meager Press is a Toronto-based publisher that specializes in interesting books of cultural, social or historic significance that are likely to be overlooked by mainstream publishing houses. Please send submissions — including a brief synopsis of the book, an author bio and chapter outlines not to exceed 1,500 words in total — to themeagerpress@gmail.com. Please do not send completed manuscripts.

www.ingramcontent.com/pod-product-compliance
Lightning Source LLC
Chambersburg PA
CBHW031621040426
42452CB00007B/614